Civil War Songbook

with historical commentary

Compiled and edited by Keith & Rusty McNeil

Companion to the recording
Civil War Songs with historical narration

WEM Records
Riverside, California

Songbooks and recordings by Keith & Rusty McNeil

Songbooks

Colonial & Revolution Songbook with historical commentary
Civil War Songbook with historical commentary

Recordings

American History Through Folksong

Colonial & Revolution Songs with historical narration
Moving West Songs with historical narration
Civil War Songs with historical narration
Cowboy Songs with historical narration
Western Railroad Songs with historical narration
Working & Union Songs with historical narration

California History Through Folksong

California Songs Volume One with historical narration
California Songs Volume Two with historical narration

Singing the Holiday Season

Folksongs for Children

Coarse & Fine

ISBN 1-878360-24-8

Contents

The War Begins

All Quiet Along the Potomac Tonight 2
Lincoln and Liberty 4
The Southern Wagon 6
God Save the South 8
Maryland, My Maryland 10
The Bonnie Blue Flag 12
Dixie's Land 14
The Yellow Rose of Texas 19
The Virginia Marseillaise 20
What's the Matter? 22
Treasury Rats 24
Yankee Doodle 26
Abraham's Daughter. 27
Ellsworth Avengers 29

The Realities of War

Just Before the Battle, Mother 32
Riding a Raid 34
Stonewall Jackson's Way 35
The Battle Hymn of the Republic 37
The Battle of Shiloh Hill 38
The Battle Cry of Freedom 40
The Southern Battle Cry of Freedom 41
Goober Peas 42
Hard Crackers Come Again No More 44
Army Grub 45
The Army Bean/Army Bugs 46
The Homespun Dress 48
We Are Coming, Father Abraham 49
Come in out of the Draft 52
We Are Coming, Father Abraham,
   Three Hundred Dollars More 54
For Bales 55

The Changing War

Kingdom Coming 58
No More Auction Block for Me 60
Slavery Chain Done Broke at Last 61
Oh, Freedom 62
Go Down Moses 63
Free at Last...65
John Brown's Body 66
Marching Song of the
   First Arkansas Regiment 68
The *Cumberland* and the *Merrimac* 70
The *Alabama* 72
Kentucky, Oh Kentucky 74
How Are You, John Morgan? 75
Tramp! Tramp! Tramp! 76
The Bonnie White Flag 78
When Johnny Comes Marching Home 80

The Union Forever

The Last Fierce Charge 82
Lorena 83
Aura Lea 85
The Children of the Battlefield 86
'Twas at the Siege of Vicksburg 88
I Goes to Fight mit Sigel 90
Old Abe Lincoln Came out of the Wilderness 92
We Are the Boys of Potomac's Ranks 93
Marching Through Georgia 94
We Are Marching on to Richmond 96
Tenting on the Old Camp Ground 98
Blue-Gray Medley 99

Introduction

The Civil War, also known as The War Between the States, was the culmination of the struggles between North and South during the nation's first one hundred years. The war was fought for many reasons: socially, slavery versus abolition; politically, states rights versus the central government; and economically, the struggle for dominance between Northern industrialism and Southern agrarianism.

Music played an important role during the war years. It served as a morale booster for the soldiers and provided an emotional outlet for soldiers' families left behind.

In mid-19th century America, music was a basic element in everyday life. People usually made their own music in their own homes. The piano was quickly becoming a standard household item, and sheet music was in great demand. When the war broke out, Americans eagerly purchased songs about the conflict. Civil War historian Kenneth Bernard estimates that the first year of the war produced about two thousand songs. Improvements in printing technology allowed music publishers to print and distribute songs quickly. Just three days after the Confederates fired on Fort Sumter, George Root's song "The First Gun is Fired" was on sale in the North. The majority of Northern songs were published as sheet music or in small paperback books. The song sheets sold for about ten cents per copy, and thousands were distributed free to the soldiers.

Soldiers usually preferred the rousing marching songs, humorous songs, protest songs and parodies that sprang spontaneously from army life. The sentimental songs, for the most part, were sung by civilians. Stephen Foster's songs were popular with everyone.

Poetry about the war was also popular, especially in the South, and poems were frequently published in Southern periodicals. Those that captured the fancy of tunesmiths were set to music, then published as songs. Northerners also wrote and published poems about the war, and some of these, too, were set to music and later published as songs.

Some of the songs included here used dialect and/or terms like "darkey" ("The Yellow Rose of Texas") and "Mick" ("The Army Bean"), which are not appropriate by today's standards. Minstrel shows and stage-Irish performers sang songs in exaggerated dialect: African ("Kingdom Coming"), Irish ("Sambo's Right To Be Kilt") and German ("I Goes to Fight mit Sigel"). Dialect songs were standard fare for humorous or "comic" songs throughout most of the 19th century, and often reflected the prejudices and insensitivity of the period. We have reproduced the lyrics in this collection as they were written and/or sung in order to preserve historical accuracy.

All songs, unless otherwise specified and credited, are traditional songs arranged and adapted by Keith & Rusty McNeil.

The War Begins

Bombardment of Fort Sumter

All Quiet Along the Potomac Tonight

In November, 1861, Harper's Weekly published a poem called "The Picket Guard." Both Ethel Beers of Goshen, New York, and Confederate Major Lamar Fontaine of Mississippi claimed to have written the words, but the weight of evidence favors Mrs. Beers' claim.

A number of composers wrote melodies to fit the poem. The tune used here, composed by John Hill Hewitt, was published in Baltimore and became popular throughout the South.

All Quiet Along the Potomac Tonight

Words: Ethel Lynn Beers. Music: John Hill Hewitt.

"All qui-et a-long the Po-to-mac to-night," Ex-cept here and there a stray pick-et Is shot as he walks on his beat to and fro, By a ri-fle-man hid in the thick-et; 'Tis noth-ing! a pri-vate or two now and then, Will not count in the news of the bat-tle, Not an of-fi-cer lost! on-ly one of the men Moan-ing out all a-lone the death rat-tle. "All qui-et a-long the Po-to-mac to-night."

"All quiet along the Potomac tonight,"
Except here and there a stray picket
Is shot as he walks on his beat to and fro,
By a rifleman hid in the thicket;
'Tis nothing! a private or two now and then,
Will not count in the news of the battle,
Not an officer lost! only one of the men
Moaning out all alone the death rattle.
"All quiet along the Potomac tonight."

There's only the sound of the lone sentry's tread,
As he tramps from the rock to the fountain,
And he thinks of the two on the low trundle bed
Far away in the cot on the mountain.
His musket falls slack — his face, dark and grim
Grows gentle with memories so tender,
As he mutters a prayer for the children asleep,
And their mother, "May heaven defend her!"
"All quiet along the Potomac tonight."

Then drawing his sleeve roughly over his eyes,
He dashes off tears that are welling,
And gathers his gun close up to his breast,
As if to keep down the heart's swelling;
He passes the fountain, the blasted pine tree,
And his footstep is lagging and weary,
Yet onward he goes, through the broad belt of light,
Toward the shades of the forest so dreary.
"All quiet along the Potomac tonight."

Hark! was it the night-wind that rustles the leaves!
Was it the moonlight so wondrously flashing?
It looked like a rifle! "Ah, Mary goodbye!"
And his life-blood is ebbing and plashing.
"All quiet along the Potomac tonight,"
No sound save the rush of the river,
While soft falls the dew on the face of the dead,
"The Picket's" off duty forever.
"All quiet along the Potomac tonight."

Lincoln and Liberty

The Republican party was born in the mid-1850's. The party nominated John C. Frémont for president in 1856. The party platform included the right of Congress to prohibit what it called "...those two relics of barbarism: polygamy and slavery." One of Frémont's campaign songs was sung to the minstrel tune "Old Dan Tucker."

Now jump aboard the Frémont train,
And soon the capitol we'll gain.
Then we'll rejoice with one in power
Who never shall to slavery cower!

Frémont carried all but five Northern states, but lost the election to James Buchanan.

Four years later, the country elected the Republican nominee, Abraham Lincoln. The Hutchinson Family, popular singers in the North during this period, helped popularize "Lincoln and Liberty." The tune is "Old Rosin the Beau," a traditional Irish folksong.

Lincoln and Liberty

Words: F. A. Simpkins. Music: anonymous.

Hurrah for the choice of the nation,
Our chieftain so brave and so true,
We'll go for the great reformation,
For Lincoln and Liberty, too!
We'll go for the son of Kentucky
The hero of Hoosierdom through,
The pride of the "Suckers" so lucky,
For Lincoln and Liberty, too!

Our David's good sling is unerring,
The Slavocrat's giant he slew,
Then shout for the freedom preferring,
For Lincoln and Liberty, too.
Then up with the banner so glorious,
The star spangled red, white and blue,
We'll fight till our banner's victorious,
For Lincoln and Liberty, too!

The Southern Wagon

Lincoln's election convinced the South that there was no way to stop Federal intervention against slavery in the territories. On December 20, 1860, just six weeks after Lincoln's election, South Carolina seceded from the Union. Mississippi, Florida, Alabama, Georgia and Louisiana seceded in January, 1861, Texas in February, and Virginia in April.

R. P. Buckley's "Wait for the Wagon" was popular in the United States during the 1850's, and its popularity continued throughout the war. Both Confederates and Unionists sang parodies of the song. "The Southern Wagon" came from the Confederacy.

The Southern Wagon

Words: anonymous. Music: R. P. Buckley.

Se - ces - sion is our watch - word, our rights we will de - mand; To de - fend our homes and fire - sides we pledge our hearts and hands. Jeff Da - vis is our pres - i - dent, with Ste - phens by his side, Brave Beau - re - gard, our gen' ral will join us in our ride.

Chorus

Wait for the wag - on, The dis - so - lu - tion wag - on, The South is our wag - on And we'll all take a ride.

Come all ye sons of freedom, and join our southern band,
We're going to fight the Yankees and drive them from our land.
Justice is our motto, and Providence our guide,
So jump into the wagon and we'll all take a ride.

CHORUS
Wait for the wagon,
The dissolution wagon,
The South is our wagon
And we'll all take a ride.

Secession is our watchword, our rights we will demand;
To defend our homes and firesides we pledge our hearts and hands.
Jeff Davis is our president, with Stephens by his side,
Brave Beauregard, our gen'ral, will join us in our ride.

Our wagon is the very best, the running gear is good.
Stuffed 'round the sides with cotton and made of Southern wood.
Carolina is the driver, with Georgia by her side.
Virginia holds the flag up while we all take a ride.

There was Tennessee and Texas also in the ring.
They would not have a government where cotton was not king.
Alabama, Florida have long ago replied;
Mississippi, Louisiana are anxious for the ride.

Missouri, North Carolina, and Arkansas are slow;
They must hurry, or we'll leave them, and then what will they do?
There's old Kentucky and Maryland won't make up their mind;
So I reckon, after all, we'll take them up behind.

Fort Sumter

God Save the South

When South Carolina seceded, Fort Sumter in Charleston Harbor was empty except for a crew of workmen who were completing construction of the fort. South Carolina wanted possession of the fort which, if properly garrisoned, might effectively control the harbor and protect the city of Charleston.

When Union Major Robert Anderson moved his troops to occupy the partially completed fort, the Confederates considered it an act of hostility. On April 12, 1861, Confederate Captain George S. James gave the order to open fire on Fort Sumter. Thirty six hours later, badly out-manned and out-gunned, Major Anderson surrendered the fort, and the Civil War began.

Both sides were confident that the war would be over within ninety days. Most enlistments were for ninety days. Northerners were convinced that when the rebels realized the Union meant business, they would back down and re-join the Union. Southerners were sure that the Yankees wouldn't fight.

Both sides knew that God was on their side.

"God Save the South" was first published in Baltimore, Maryland. George Miles, who wrote the words, published them under the name Earnest Halphin, in 1861. The song remained popular in the South throughout the war.

Montgomery, Alabama, February 8, 1861

God Save the South

Words: George H. Miles. Music: Charles W. A. Ellerbrock.

God save the South, God save the South,
Her altars and firesides, God save the South!
Now that the war is nigh, now that we arm to die,
Chanting our battle cry, Freedom or death!
Chanting our battle cry, Freedom or death!

God be our shield, at home or afield,
Stretch thine arm over us, strengthen and save.
What though they're three to one, forward each sire and son,
Strike till the war is won, strike to the grave!
Strike till the war is won, strike to the grave!

God made the right, stronger than might,
Millions would trample us down in their pride.
Lay Thou their legions low, roll back the ruthless foe,
Let the proud spoiler know God's on our side,
Let the proud spoiler know God's on our side.

Hark honor's call, summoning all,
Summoning all of us unto the strife.
Songs of the South awake! Strike till the brand shall break,
Strike for dear Honor's sake, Freedom and Life!
Strike for dear Honor's sake, Freedom and Life!

Rebels before our fathers of yore,
Rebel's the righteous name Washington bore.
Why, then, be ours the same,
the name that he snatched from shame,
Making it first in fame, foremost in war.
Making it first in fame, foremost in war.

War to the hilt, theirs be the guilt,
Who fetter the free man to ransom the slave,
Up then, and undismayed, sheathe not the battle blade
Till the last foe is laid low in the grave!
Till the last foe is laid low in the grave!

God save the South, God save the South,
Dry the dim eyes that now follow our path.
Still let the light feet rove safe through the orange grove;
Still keep the land we love safe from Thy wrath,
Still keep the land we love safe from Thy wrath.

God save the South, God save the South,
Her altars and firesides, God save the South!
For the great war is nigh, and we will win or die,
Chanting our battle cry, Freedom or death!
Chanting our battle cry, Freedom or death!

Maryland, My Maryland

James Randall, a native of Baltimore, was in Louisiana when he heard the news of fighting in his native city in April, 1861. He immediately wrote the poem "Maryland, My Maryland," and it was published in the New Orleans Delta on April 26. Miss Jennie Cary of Baltimore set Randall's poem to the tune of a then popular college song "Lauriger Horatius" (the melody originally came from the German Christmas carol "O Tannenbaum"). Miller and Beacham published the song in Baltimore in 1861. The piano score on the original sheet music was arranged by Charles Ellerbrock, who adapted the music for "God Save the South."

Maryland, My Maryland

Words: James Ryder Randall. Music: anonymous.

The despot's heel is on thy shore, Maryland! My Maryland!
His touch is at thy temple door, Maryland! My Maryland!
Avenge the patriotic gore that flecked the streets of Baltimore,
And be the Battle Queen of yore, Maryland! My Maryland!

Hark to a wandering Son's appeal! Maryland! My Maryland!
My Mother State! to thee I kneel, Maryland! My Maryland!
For life and death, for woe and weal, thy peerless chivalry reveal,
And gird thy beauteous limbs with steel, Maryland! My Maryland!

Thou wilt not cower in the dust, Maryland! My Maryland!
Thy beaming sword shall never rust, Maryland! My Maryland!
Remember Carroll's sacred trust, remember Howard's warlike thrust,
And all thy slumberers with the just, Maryland! My Maryland!

Come! for thy shield is bright and strong, Maryland! My Maryland!
Come! for thy dalliance, does thee wrong, Maryland! My Maryland!
Come! to thine own heroic throng, that stalks with Liberty along,
And give a new Key to thy song, Maryland! My Maryland!

Dear Mother! burst the tyrant's chain, Maryland! My Maryland!
Virginia should not call in vain! Maryland! My Maryland!
She meets her sisters on the plain "Sic semper" 'tis the proud refrain,
That baffles minions back amain, Maryland! My Maryland!

I see the blush upon thy cheek, Maryland! My Maryland!
But thou wast ever bravely meek, Maryland! My Maryland!
But lo! there surges forth a shriek from hill to hill, from creek to creek,
Potomac calls to Chesapeake, Maryland! My Maryland!

Thou wilt not yield the vandal toll, Maryland! My Maryland!
Thou wilt not crook to his control, Maryland! My Maryland!
Better the fire upon thee roll, better the blade! the shot, the bowl,
Than crucifixion of the soul, Maryland! My Maryland!

I hear the distant thunder-hum, Maryland! My Maryland!
The Old Line's bugle, fife and drum, Maryland! My Maryland!
She is not dead, nor deaf nor dumb, huzza!
She spurns the Northern scum!
She breathes, she burns! she'll come! she'll come!
Maryland! My Maryland!

Despite the sentiments expressed in Randall's song, Maryland, a slave state, remained in the Union. An anonymous writer wrote an answer to "Maryland, My Maryland."

The Rebel feet are on our shore, Maryland, my Maryland!
I smell 'em half a mile or more, Maryland, my Maryland!
Their shockless hordes are at my door,
Their drunken generals on my floor,
What now can sweeten Baltimore? Maryland, my Maryland!

First blood – The Sixth Massachusetts Regiment fighting their way through Baltimore, April 19, 1861

The Bonnie Blue Flag

The most stirring Confederate songs were written early in the war when Southern confidence was running high. Harry Macarthy composed "The Bonnie Blue Flag" during the first year of the war. Sung to the tune of the old Irish song "The Irish Jaunting Car," his song was second only to "Dixie" in popularity among Confederate soldiers. Macarthy was born in England. He became a vaudeville performer in the United States, calling himself the "Arkansas Comedian."

There is a legend that when Union General Benjamin F. Butler was commander in New Orleans, he banned "The Bonnie Blue Flag," fined anyone who sang it $25, fined the publisher $500 and confiscated the plates from the printer.

Jefferson Davis

The Bonnie Blue Flag

Words: Harry Macarthy. Music: anonymous.

We are a band of brothers, and native to the soil,
Fighting for our liberty, with treasure, blood and toil;
And when our rights were threatened, the cry rose near and far,
Hurrah for the Bonnie Blue Flag, that bears a Single Star!

CHORUS:
Hurrah! Hurrah! for Southern Rights Hurrah!
Hurrah! for the Bonnie Blue Flag that bears a Single Star!

As long as the Union was faithful to her trust,
Like friends and brethren kind were we and just;
But now when Northern treachery attempts our rights to mar,
We hoist on high the Bonnie Blue Flag that bears a Single Star.

First, gallant South Carolina nobly made the stand;
Then came Alabama, who took her by the hand;
Next, quickly Mississippi, then Georgia, Florida;
All raised on high the Bonnie Blue Flag that bears a Single Star.

Ye men of valor, gather 'round the Banner of the Right,
Texas and fair Louisiana, join us in the fight;
With Davis, our loved President, and Stephens, Statesman rare,
We'll rally 'round the Bonnie Blue Flag that bears a Single Star.

And here's to brave Virginia! the Old Dominion State;
With the young Confederacy she has linked her fate.
Impelled by her example, now other states prepare
To hoist on high the Bonnie Blue Flag that bears a Single Star.

Then cheer, boys, cheer, raise the joyous shout,
Arkansas and North Carolina now have both gone out;
And let another rousing cheer for Tennessee be given,
The Single Star of the Bonnie Blue Flag has grown to be Eleven.

Then here's to our Confederacy, strong we are and brave,
Like patriots of old, we'll fight our heritage to save;
And rather than submit to shame, to die we would prefer,
So cheer for the Bonnie Blue Flag that bears a Single Star.

Dixie's Land

The anthem of the Confederacy was "Dixie," written in 1859 by Northerner Dan Decatur Emmett, the king of the minstrel songwriters. Emmett wrote "Dixie" for a minstrel troupe called "Bryant's Minstrels." Other Emmett songs that entered the oral tradition include "The Blue Tailed Fly" and "Old Dan Tucker."

"Dixie" made its Southern debut in New Orleans. It was also played at Jefferson Davis's inauguration at Montgomery, Alabama, on February 16, 1861.

Dixie's Land

Words and music: Dan Decatur Emmett.

I wish I was in the land of cot - ton, Old times there are not for - got - ten; Look a - way! Look a - way! Look a - way! Dix - ie Land. In Dix - ie Land where I was born in, Ear - ly on one frost - y morn - in' Look a - way! Look a - way! Look a - way! Dix - ie Land.

Chorus

I wish I was in Dix - ie, Hoo - ray! Hoo - ray! In Dix - ie Land, I'll take my stand, To

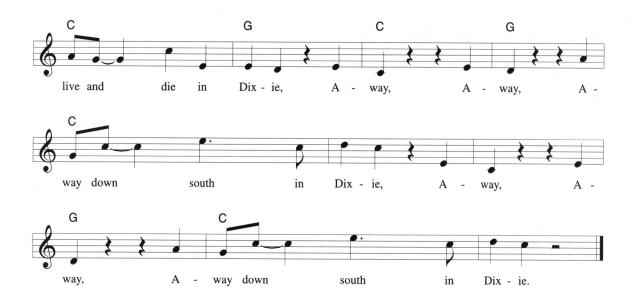

live and die in Dix - ie, A - way, A - way, A -

way down south in Dix - ie, A - way, A -

way, A - way down south in Dix - ie.

I wish I was in the land of cotton,
Old times there are not forgotten;
Look away! Look away! Look away! Dixie Land.
In Dixie Land where I was born in,
Early on one frosty mornin'
Look away! Look away! Look away! Dixie Land.

CHORUS
I wish I was in Dixie, Hooray! Hooray!
In Dixie Land, I'll take my stand,
To live and die in Dixie,
Away, Away, Away down south in Dixie,
Away, Away, Away down south in Dixie.

Old Missus married "Will-the-weaver,"
William was a gay deceiver;
Look away! Look away! Look away! Dixie Land.
But when he put his arm around her,
He smiled as fierce as a forty pounder.
Look away! Look away! Look away! Dixie Land.

His face was as sharp as a butcher's cleaver
But that did not seem to grieve her;
Look away! (etc.)
Old Missus acted the foolish part,
And died for a man that broke her heart.
Look away! (etc.)

Now here's a health to the next old Missus,
And all the girls that want to kiss us;
Look away! (etc.)
But if you want to drive away sorrow,
Come and hear this song tomorrow.
Look away! (etc.)

There's buck-wheat cakes and "Ingen" batter,
Makes you fat or a little fatter;
Look away! (etc.)
Then hoe it down and scratch your gravel,
To Dixie Land I'm bound to travel.
Look away! (etc.)

Southerners wrote more parodies of "Dixie" than any other song during the war. In Arkansas they sang:

Dixie's Land (Arkansas Parody)

Music: Dan Decatur Emmett. Words: anonymous

Southrons hear your country call you,
Up lest worse than death befall you,
To arms, to arms, to arms in Dixie.
For faith betrayed, pledges broken,
wrongs inflicted, insults spoken,
To arms, to arms, to arms in Dixie.

Advance the flag of Dixie, Hurrah! Hurrah!
For Dixie's Land we'll take our stand
To live or die for Dixie,
To arms, to arms, and conquer peace for Dixie.
To arms, to arms, and conquer peace for Dixie.

In Texas they sang:

Dixie's Land (Texas Parody)

Music: Dan Decatur Emmett. Words: anonymous

One night when we was gettin' dry, A little old whiskey was the cry, A-way, a-way, a-way down South in Texas. The boys hit up, they had a plan To rob the commissary man. A-way, a-way, a-way down South in Texas. Oh when we get the whiskey a-way, a-way, We'll drink old rum and think we're home A-way down South in Texas. A-

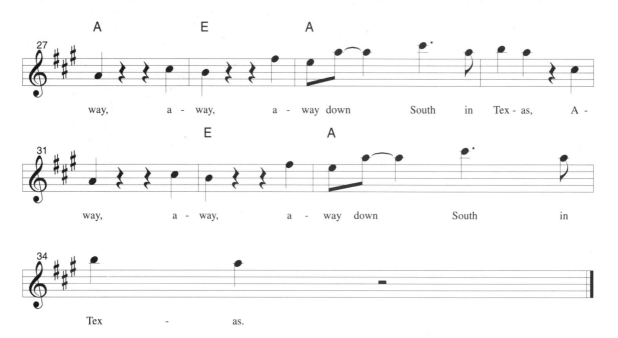

way,   a - way,   a - way down   South   in   Tex - as,   A -

way,   a - way,   a - way down   South   in

Tex -   as.

One night when we was gettin' dry,
A little old whiskey was the cry,
Away, away, away down South in Texas.
The boys hit up, they had a plan
To rob the commissary man.
Away, away, away down South in Texas.

Oh when we get the whiskey away, away,
We'll drink old rum and think we're home
Away down South in Texas.
Away, away, away down South in Texas.

Montgomery, Alabama: First seat of the Rebel government

The Yellow Rose of Texas

Another minstrel song, especially popular among Texas soldiers, was "The Yellow Rose of Texas." The term "yellow" in the song refers to a light-skinned African-American, probably of mixed African and European ancestry.

The Yellow Rose of Texas

Words and music: anonymous.

There's a yel-low rose in Tex-as that I am going to see, No oth-er dar-key knows her, no dar-key on-ly me, She cried so when I left her it like to broke my heart, And if I ev-er find her, we nev-er more will part.

There's a yellow rose in Texas that I am going to see,
No other darkey knows her, no darkey only me,
She cried so when I left her it like to broke my heart,
And if I ever find her, we never more will part.

CHORUS
She's the sweetest rose of color this darkey ever knew,
Her eyes are bright as diamonds, they sparkle like the dew,
You may talk about your dearest May, and sing of Rosa Lee,
But the Yellow Rose of Texas beats the belles of Tennessee.

Where the Rio Grande is flowing, and the starry skies are bright,
She walks along the river in the quiet summer night;
She thinks if I remember when we parted long ago,
I promised to come back again and not to leave her so.

Oh, now I'm going to find her for my heart is full of woe,
And we'll sing the song together that we sang so long ago;
We'll play the banjo gaily, and we'll sing the songs of yore,
And the Yellow Rose of Texas shall be mine for ever more.

The Virginia Marseillaise

French-Americans in New Orleans contributed a number of songs to the Confederate cause. Some of the most effective used the powerful melody from the French revolution, the "Marseillaise." The "Marseillaise" became so strongly identified with the Confederacy that a French theatrical group was arrested in New York for singing it during their performance.

The "Virginia Marseillaise" was also known as the "Southern Marseillaise."

The Virginia Marseillaise

Words: F. W. Rosier. Music: Rouget de L'isle

Virginia hears the dreadful summons, sounding hoarsely from afar:
On her sons she calls and calmly bids them now prepare for war,
Bids them now prepare for war.
With manly hearts, and hands to aid her, she cares not how her foemen swarm,
She bares her bosom to the storm: while she laughs to scorn the proud invader.
To arms! brothers dear; gird on the trenchant brand!
Strike home! Strike home! No craven fear! For home and native land!
Strike home! Strike home! No craven fear! For home and native land!

Shall the sons of Old Virginia prove unworthy of their sires?
No! they'll show the haughty foemen that in fight, she "never tires,"
That in fight, she "never tires."
With favoring Heaven to befriend her. To whom alone she bends the knee,
'Till every foot of soil is free, she her sacred cause will ne'er surrender,
To arms! (etc.)

A ray of never dying glory shall Virginia's brow o'erspread;
Men unborn shall tell the story, how their fathers fought and bled,
How their fathers fought and bled.
While fairest hands their wounds were tending. And brightest eyes the dear bewailed,
How not a noble bosom quailed, e'en to die, their native land defending.
To arms! (etc.)

O liberty! can man resign thee, who has felt thy generous flame?
Can dungeons, bolts and bars confine thee, or whips thy noble spirit tame?
Or whips thy noble spirit tame?
Too long the world has wept, bewailing the savage power that conquerors wield,
But Freedom is our sword and shield, and all their arts are unavailing.
To arms! (etc.)

Long be it thus, may we forever for Freedom brave the battle storm;
Rise in her might, and rising, sever the bonds that tyrant bands would form.
Sever the bonds that tyrant bands would form.
Then plume and steel in sunbeams glancing, shall show where Freedom's banners float,
And thrilling to the trumpet's note, we'll see her warrior sons advancing.
To arms! (etc.)

What's the Matter?

As the country was dividing, differences of opinion, loyalties and politics intensified on both sides of the Mason-Dixon Line. Within a week after the surrender of Fort Sumter, the Richmond Illumination was held to celebrate secession. Citizens formed torchlight processions. Homes and businesses that remained dark during the Illumination were branded Abolitionist, Yankee or Black Republican, and ostracized.

In the North, Southern sympathizers were called "copperheads," named after a poisonous snake. The copperheads created problems for the Union throughout the war, and feelings against copperheads ran high.

What's the Matter?

Words and music: Charles Boynton.

See the people turning out, what, what's the matter?
What is all this noise about? What, what's the matter?
Gathered in from far and near, every loyal man is here,
What is it the people fear? What, what's the matter?

CHORUS
What, what's the matter now, what, what's the matter?
What's the cause of all this row? What, what's the matter?

Traitors in our midst we've found, that's what's the matter,
Peddling here their treason 'round, that's what's the matter.
Men that to our foes have cried, "You can count us on your side,
We will let the Union slide," That's what's the matter.

CHORUS
That's what's the matter now, that's what's the matter;
Treason here we won't allow, that's what's the matter!

Firing on our armies' rear, trying to scatter
Disaffection far and near, that's what's the matter.
"Take your proclamation back, take your armies off the track."
Cry aloud this Tory pack, that's what's the matter.

CHORUS
That's what's the matter now, that's what's the matter
Treason here we won't allow, that's what's the matter.

Hear ye what the people say, "Stop now your clatter,
Uncle Sam will win the day, that's what's the matter.
If he wants a million men let him tell us where, and when,
They'll be ready there, and then." That's what's the matter.

CHORUS
That's what's the matter, ho! That's what's the matter -
Every drafted man shall go, that's what's the matter.

Treasury Rats

Most Southerners believed that the Yankees were corrupt, selfish profit-seekers who would not put up a good fight. Most Northerners believed that the evils of slavery had created a South full of degraded slave-drivers who would back down when confronted by the Union army. In reality, they were about equal in the human qualities of morality and corruption, patriotism and disloyalty.

However, there were important differences militarily: Northerners outnumbered Southerners five to two. Two-thirds of the nation's railroad mileage traversed Northern soil. The North controlled the majority of the Atlantic

shipping trade. Northerners held much more wealth in property and capital, and had ten times more productive capacity than the South. On the other hand, the South was producing more corn and livestock than the North. Southern rivers, swamps and mountains provided natural fortifications, and the South was the major world supplier of cotton.

Both sides began the war with empty treasuries. When Union Treasury Secretary Salmon P. Chase suggested using paper money, Northerners reacted with anger and derision.

Treasury Rats

Words and music: anonymous.

Treas-ur-y Rats are swarm-ing a-round, ev-'ry-where o-ver and un-der the ground, In all the hous-es and all the shops, from cel-lar floors to gar-ret tops, Oh, con-found the Treas-ur-y Rats! Go to Wash-ing-ton, clap your ear to the Treas-ur-y Vault, and there you'll hear, Ev-'ry mo-ment of night and day, ten thou-sand rats all gnaw-ing a-way! Hun-dreds of pres-ses, of high steam power,

Treasury rats are swarming around, everywhere over and under the ground,
In all the houses and all the shops, from cellar floors to garret tops,
Oh, confound the Treasury Rats!
Go to Washington, clap your ear to the Treasury Vault, and there you'll hear,
Every moment of night and day, ten thousand rats all gnawing away!
Hundreds of presses, at high steam power, print the "money" these rats devour,
And if "Copperheads" try to scare them away, "Hush!" - the government papers say,
Oh, confound the Treasury Rats!

Treasury Rats are hungry enough! Nothing on earth can be too tough,
Nothing too hard, or soft, or sweet, or heavy, or light, for them to eat.
Oh, confound the Treasury Rats!
Shoddy for blankets, coats and hats, is just the thing for Treasury Rats;
O'er ironclads they lick their lips, and countless fleets of rotten ships.
Ammunition, shot, and shell, horses in numbers none can tell,
Cannon and rifles, powder and ball, these ravenous vermin gobble them all.
Oh, confound the Treasury Rats!

Down on the battle field I stood, where brethren had shed each other's blood,
And armies of Rats were moving 'round, hither and thither over the ground,
Oh, confound the Treasury Rats!
I looked and I saw their snouts were red, as they gorged themselves from off the dead;
They stroked their whiskers, and switched their tails, and danced for joy in the tainted gales!
They tore the flesh from the dead men's bones,
and chattered and squealed, 'mid the wounded's groans,
"Sure 'tis a nation's noblest bliss to keep us Rats in victuals like this!"
Oh, confound the Treasury Rats!

Treasury Rats now rule the land! Everything moves by their command,
They cut out the work, and handle the pay, and a charming song they sing today.
Oh, confound the Treasury Rats!
Traitors and Copperheads, penniless knaves, you are the stuff to fill soldiers' graves!
The country's great and only need is that we shall make money, while you shall bleed!
This is true 'loyalty' - on with the war! And this is what you are fighting it for!
Go on killing each other - gloriously - till we are as rich as we'd like to be!"
Oh, confound the Treasury Rats!

Coming events cast shadows before! The reign of the Rats will soon be o'er;
Some already have left the ship, and others will soon be giving the slip.
Oh, confound the Treasury Rats!
Water they hate, and water they fear, and water will soon be everywhere;
From West and East and South and North rivers of wrath are rolling forth.
Tides are rising, mighty in power, higher and higher, hour by hour,
And, when November has come for good, with one, vast overwhelming flood,
We'll drown out the Treasury Rats!

Salmon P. Chase

Yankee Doodle

Printing paper money turned out to be much more damaging to the South than to the North. The North raised 13 percent of its income from printing paper money - the South raised 60 percent from paper money. Confederate prices eventually inflated to nearly one hundred times their original level, causing great economic distress.

Except for the dissenters, most Northerners and Southerners entered the war with enthusiasm for their respective causes. Enlistments were running so high that there weren't enough weapons to arm the recruits. Some of the volunteer regiments were quite colorful, like the 79th New York Highlanders with their kilts and bagpipes.

Union troops marched to a number of tunes from the American Revolution. Two of the favorites were "Hail Columbia" and "Yankee Doodle."

Yankee Doodle (setting for Highland bagpipes)

Music: anonymous.

Abraham's Daughter

The most colorful of the newly formed regiments were the Zouaves. They wore bright red baggy pants, short vests trimmed with gold braid, and brightly colored turbans or caps with tassels. Their uniforms were patterned after those worn by the Zouaves from the Jurjua Mountains in Algeria, legendary fighters who served in the French army.

"Abraham's Daughter," also known as "The Raw Recruit," was very popular in the North. Soldiers wrote parodies of it, and minstrel troupes sang it everywhere. In the song, the words "I belong to the Fire Zou Zous" refer to the New York Fire Zouaves. The Fire Zouaves were recruited from New York's volunteer firemen.

Septimus Winner, who wrote "Abraham's Daughter," was a Northern Democrat. Later in the war he composed a song in defense of General George B. McClellan, whom Lincoln had just relieved as commander of the Union armies. Winner was accused of treason for writing that song.

The American favorites "Oh, Where, Oh Where Has My Little Dog Gone?" and "Listen to the Mockingbird" were also composed by Septimus Winner.

A Zouave at Washington

Abraham's Daughter

Words and music: Septimus Winner.

Oh! kind folks listen to my song, it is no idle story,
It's all about a volunteer who's goin' to fight for glory;
Now don't you think that I am right? For I am nothing shorter.
And I belong to the Fire Zou Zous, and don't you think I oughter,
We're goin' down to Washington to fight for Abraham's daughter.

Oh! should you ask me who she am, Columbia is her name, sir,
She is the child of Abraham or Uncle Sam, the same, sir.
Now if I fight, why ain't I right? And don't you think I oughter.
The volunteers are pouring in from every loyal quarter,
And I'm goin' 'long to Washington to fight for Abraham's daughter.

They say we have no officers, but ah! they are mistaken;
And soon you'll see the rebels run. With all the fuss they're makin';
For there is one who just sprung up, he'll show the foe no quarter,
(McClellan is the man I mean), you know he hadn't oughter,
For he's gone down to Washington to fight for Abraham's daughter.

We'll have a spree with Johnny Bull, perhaps, some day or other,
And won't he have his fingers full, if not a deal of bother;
For Yankee boys are just the lads upon the land or water;
And won't we have a "bully" fight, and don't you think we oughter,
If he is caught at any time, insulting Abraham's daughter.

But let us lay all jokes aside, it is a sorry question;
The man who would these States divide should hang for his suggestion.
One Country and one Flag, I say, whoe'er the war may slaughter;
So I'm goin' as a Fire Zou-a, and don't you think I oughter,
I'm goin' down to Washington to fight for Abraham's daughter.

Ellsworth Avengers

The Zouaves suffered one of the first Northern casualties of the war. On May 24, 1861, twenty-four year old Colonel Elmer Ellsworth, commander of the 11th Regiment of the New York Fire Zouaves, was shot while taking down the Confederate flag in Alexandria, Virginia. Ellsworth was a patent attorney, and had helped recruit the New York Fire Zouaves. His death received national attention, and made him a martyr for the Union cause. He was also a favorite of Abraham Lincoln, and his funeral services were held in the East Room of the White House, attended by the President and First Lady.

Elmer E. Ellsworth

Ellsworth Avengers

Words: anonymous. Music: H. R. Thompson.

Down where the patriot army, near Potomac's side,
Guards the glorious cause of freedom, gallant Ellsworth died;
Brave was the noble Chieftain, at his country's call,
Hastened to the field of battle and was first to fall.

CHORUS
Strike, freemen, for the Union, sheath your swords no more;
While remains in arms a traitor, on Columbia's shore.

Entering the traitor city with his soldiers true,
Leading up the Zouave columns, fixed became his view.
See that rebel flag is floating o'er yon building tall!
Spoke he, while his dark eye glistened, "Boys, that flag must fall!"

Quickly from its proud position that base flag was torn,
Trampled 'neath the feet of freemen, circling Ellsworth's form;
See him bear it down the landing, past the traitor's door,
Hear him groan; Oh! God, they've shot him, Ellsworth is no more.

First to fall, thou youthful martyr, hapless was thy fate;
Hastened we as thy avengers from thy native state.
Speed we on from town and city, not for wealth or fame;
But because we love the Union, and our Ellsworth name.

Traitors' hands shall never sunder that for which you died;
Hear the oath our lips now utter, those our nation's pride.
By our hopes of yon bright heaven, by the land we love,
By the God who reigns above us, we'll avenge thy blood.

The Realities of War

The Fort Pillow Massacre

Just Before the Battle, Mother

A partner in the music publishing firm Root and Cady, George Root composed and published many of the Union's favorite songs. In "Just Before the Battle, Mother," he makes reference to his popular "Battle Cry of Freedom."

Just Before the Battle, Mother

Words and music: George Frederick Root.

Just before the battle, Mother,
I am thinking most of you.
While upon the field we're watching,
With the enemy in view.
Comrades brave are 'round me lying,
Filled with thoughts of home and God;
For well they know that on the morrow,
Some will sleep beneath the sod.

CHORUS
Farewell, Mother, you may never
Press me to your heart again;
But oh, you'll not forget me, Mother,
If I'm numbered with the slain.

Oh, I long to see you, Mother,
And the loving ones at home,
But I'll never leave our banner
Till in honor I can come.
Tell the traitors, all around you,
That their cruel words, we know,
In every battle kill our soldiers
By the help they give the foe.

Hark! I hear the bugles sounding,
'Tis the signal for the fight,
Now may God protect us, Mother,
As He ever does the right.
Hear the "Battle Cry of Freedom."
How it swells upon the air,
Oh, yes we'll rally 'round the standard
Or we'll perish nobly there.

"Just Before the Battle, Mother" was popular in
the South as well as the North. Southerners sang
this parody:

Just before the battle, mother,
I was drinking mountain dew,
When I saw the Rebels marching,
To the rear I quickly flew,
Where the stragglers were flying,
Thinking of their homes and wives.
'Twas not the Rebs we feared, dear mother,
But our own dear precious lives.

Dragging artillery over the mountains

Riding a Raid

The first major battle of the Civil War took place at Manassas, Virginia, on July 21, 1861. In the North it was known as the Battle of Bull Run, named for a nearby creek. The battle was fought on a Sunday, and many Northerners - men, women, children, senators and congressmen - came with wine and food to picnic while watching the Yanks whip the Rebels. The Union, however, suffered a humiliating defeat. As the soldiers retreated, the spectators retreated, too, blocking the routes. The result was panic among both soldiers and civilians.

Among the Confederate officers who distinguished themselves at Bull Run were Stonewall Jackson and Jeb Stuart. Both men became legends. The handsome cavalry leader General James Ewell Brown "Jeb" Stuart kept a personal banjo picker on his staff. "Riding a Raid" was a tribute to General Stuart. The tune is "Bonnie Dundee," a Scots song and pipe tune.

James E. B. Stuart

Riding a Raid

Words and music: anonymous.

'Tis Stone-wall, the re-bel that leans on his sword, And while we are mount-ing prays low to the Lord; "Now each cav-a-lier that loves Hon-or and Right, let him fol-low the feath-er of Stu-art to-night."

Chorus

Come tight-en your girth, slack-en your rein, Buck-le your blan-ket and hol-ster a-gain. Try the click of your trig-ger and bal-ance your blade, For he must ride sure that goes rid-ing a raid.

'Tis Stonewall, the Rebel, that leans on his sword,
And while we are mounting, prays low to the Lord:
"Now each cavalier that loves Honor and Right,
Let him follow the feather of Stuart tonight."

CHORUS
Come tighten your girth, slacken your rein,
Buckle your blanket and holster again.
Try the click of your trigger and balance your blade,
For he must ride sure that goes riding a raid.

Now gallop, now gallop, to swim or to ford!
Old Stonewall, still watching, prays low to the Lord,
"Goodbye dear old Rebel! the river's not wide,
And Maryland's lights in her window to guide."

There's a man in a white house with blood on his mouth!
If there's knaves in the North, there are braves in the South.
We are three thousand horses, and not one afraid,
We are three thousand sabres and not a dull blade.

Then gallop, then gallop, by ravines and rocks!
Who would bar us the way take his toll in hard knocks.
For with these points of steel, on the line of Penn,
We have made some fine strokes - and we'll make 'em again.

Stonewall Jackson's Way

Thomas Jonathan Jackson earned his nickname "Stonewall" at Manassas. He outfought a number of Union generals in the Shenandoah Valley, as well as in Manassas, Antietam and Fredericksburg. He was Robert E. Lee's most effective officer.

Famous for his swift attacks, hard fighting and firm religious convictions, Jackson prayed before and after every battle. A devout Presbyterian, his demeanor reflected both a fear and a love of God, and a definite singleness of purpose. His religious fervor eventually caused gossip among his soldiers. They described him as "a body full of light," and called him (not to his face) "Old Blue Light," or "The Blue Light Elder." Ironically, Jackson was accidentally shot by his own men at Chancellorsville, Virginia. He died May 10, 1863.

John Palmer, the author of "Stonewall Jackson's Way," was a reporter. Palmer wrote the song while covering the battle at Antietam (Sharpsburg). In the song, the line "Hill's at the ford" refers to General A. P. Hill who served under Jackson's command, and after Jackson's death replaced him as commander of the Second Corps.

Thomas Jonathan Jackson

Stonewall Jackson's Way

Words: John Williamson Palmer. Music: anonymous.

Come, stack arms, men, pile on the rails, stir up the camp-fire bright; No matter if the canteen fails, we'll make a roaring night. Here Shenandoah crawls along, hear burly Blue Ridge echoes strong, To swell the brigade's rousing song, of "Stonewall Jackson's way."

Come, stack arms, men, pile on the rails, stir up the camp-fire bright;
No matter if the canteen fails, we'll make a roaring night.
Here Shenandoah crawls along, hear burly Blue Ridge echoes strong,
To swell the brigade's rousing song, of "Stonewall Jackson's way."

We see him now, the old slouched hat couched o'er his eye askew,
The shrewd, dry smile, the speech so pat, so calm, so blunt, so true.
The "Blue Light Elder" knows 'em well, says he,
"That's Banks, he's fond of shell,
Lord, save his soul! we'll give him —
well", that's "Stonewall Jackson's way."

Silence! Ground arms! Kneel all! Caps off!
old "Blue Light's" going to pray.
Strangle the fool that dares to scoff! Attention! It's his way!
Appealing from his native sod, "Hear us, Almighty God!
Lay bare thine arm, stretch forth thy rod, Amen!"
That's "Stonewall Jackson's way."

He's in the saddle now! Fall in! Steady! The whole brigade!
Hill's at the ford, cut off; we'll win his way out ball and blade.
What matter if our shoes are worn? What matter if our feet are torn?
Quick step! we're with him ere the dawn!
That's "Stonewall Jackson's way."

The sun's bright lances rout the mists of morning - and, by George!
Here's Longstreet, struggling in the lists, hemmed in an ugly gorge.
Pope and his Yankees, whipped before;
"Bayonets and grape!" hear Stonewall's roar.
"Charge, Stuart! pay off Ashby's score," is "Stonewall Jackson's way."

Ah! maiden, wait, and watch, and yearn for news of Stonewall's band!
Ah! widow, read - with eyes that burn - that ring upon thy hand!
Ah! wife, sew on, hope on, and pray! that life shall not be all forlorn -
The foe had better ne'er been born that gets in Stonewall's way.

The Battle Hymn of the Republic

The disastrous defeat at Manassas shocked the North. Lincoln replaced Winfield Scott with George B. McClellan as commanding general of the Union armies. Northern enthusiasm for the war faded.

The sagging morale received a boost when Harper's Magazine printed "The Battle Hymn of the Republic" in February, 1862. The words were written by feminist-abolitionist Julia Ward Howe, and she set them to the tune of "John Brown's Body."

In her autobiography "Reminiscences," Julia Ward Howe writes: "My...minister was in the carriage with me, as were several other friends...we sang snatches of the army songs so popular...concluding with 'John Brown's body lies a-mouldring in the ground; His soul is marching on.'...Mr. Clarke said, 'Mrs. Howe, why do you not write some good words for that stirring tune?'...I awoke in the gray of the morning twilight: and...the long lines of the desired poem began to twine themselves in my mind...I sprang out of bed, and...scrawled the verses almost without looking at the paper."

Her "Battle Hymn" gained immediate and lasting popularity among soldiers and civilians.

The Battle Hymn of the Republic

Words: Julia Ward Howe. Music: anonymous.

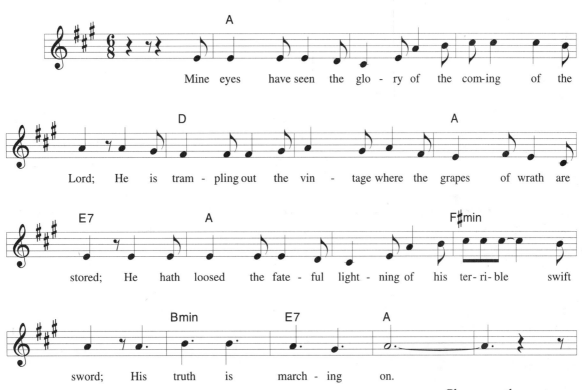

Chorus on the next page

Mine eyes have seen the glory of the coming of the Lord:
He is trampling out the vintage where the grapes of wrath are stored;
He hath loosed the fateful lightning of His terrible swift sword:
His truth is marching on.

CHORUS
Glory! Glory Hallelujah! Glory! Glory Hallelujah!
Glory! Glory Hallelujah! His truth is marching on.

I have seen Him in the watch-fires of a hundred circling camps,
They have builded Him an altar in the evening dews and damps;
I can read His righteous sentence by the dim and flaring lamps:
His day is marching on.

I have read a fiery gospel writ in burnished rows of steel:
"As ye deal with my contemners, so with you my grace shall deal;"
Let the Hero born of woman crush the serpent with his heel,
Since God is marching on.

He has sounded forth the trumpet that shall never call retreat;
He is sifting out the hearts of men before His judgment seat:
Oh, be swift, my soul, to answer Him! be jubilant, my feet!
Our God is marching on.

In the beauty of the lilies Christ was born across the sea,
With a glory in his bosom that transfigures you and me:
As He died to make men holy, let us die to make men free,
While God is marching on.

Chorus

Glo — ry! Glo — ry Hal — le — lu — — jah!

D   A

Glo — ry! Glo — ry Hal — le — lu — jah!

F#min

Glo — ry! Glo — ry Hal — le — lu — jah! His

Bmin   E7   A

truth   is   march — ing   on.

The Battle of Shiloh Hill

The battle at Shiloh, Tennessee, in April, 1862, brought home to both sides the bloody cost of the war. Over 20,000 Confederate and Union soldiers were killed or wounded. Some Confederate leaders claimed victory at Shiloh. In reality, the lack of a Confederate victory at Shiloh, plus the fall of Island Number Ten on the Mississippi River, spelled the doom of the Confederate West.

M. B. Smith, who wrote the words to the song, served in Company C, 2nd Regiment, Texas Volunteers. In contrast to most of the songs about battles, this Confederate song makes no judgmental statement about the enemy. Instead, the song effectively describes the realities of war: killing, suffering and dying. "The Battle of Shiloh Hill" remains a part of the oral tradition in the Southern Appalachian mountains.

The Battle of Shiloh Hill

Words: M. B. Smith. Music: anonymous.

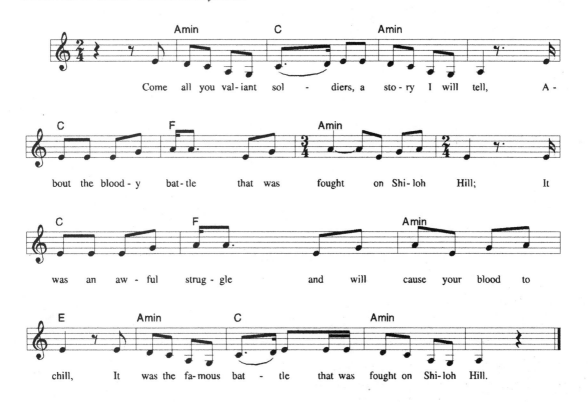

Come all you valiant soldiers, a story I will tell, A-bout the bloody battle that was fought on Shiloh Hill; It was an awful struggle and will cause your blood to chill, It was the famous battle that was fought on Shiloh Hill.

Come all you valiant soldiers, a story I will tell,
About the bloody battle that was fought on Shiloh Hill;
It was an awful struggle and will cause your blood to chill,
It was the famous battle that was fought on Shiloh Hill.

It was the sixth of April just at the break of day,
The drums and fifes were playing for us to march away;
The feeling of that hour I do remember still,
For the wounded and the dying that lay on Shiloh Hill.

About the hour of sunrise the battle it began,
And before the day had vanished we fought them hand to hand;
The horrors of the field did my heart with anguish fill,
For the wounded and the dying that lay on Shiloh Hill.

There were men from every nation, laid on those bloody plains,
Fathers, sons and brothers were numbered with the slain,
That has caused so many homes with deep mourning to be filled,
All from the bloody battle that was fought on Shiloh Hill.

The wounded men were crying for help from everywhere,
While others, who were dying were offering God their prayer,
"Protect my wife and children if it is Thy holy will!"
Such were the prayers I heard that night on Shiloh Hill.

And early the next morning we were called to arms again,
Unmindful of the wounded and unmindful of the slain,
The struggle was renewed and ten thousand men were killed;
This was the second conflict of the famous Shiloh Hill.

The battle it raged on, though dead and dying men
Lay thick all o'er the ground, on the hill and on the glen;
And from their deadly wounds the blood ran like a rill;
Such were the mournful sights that I saw on Shiloh Hill.

Before the day was ended, the battle ceased to roar,
And thousands of brave soldiers had fell to rise no more;
They left their vacant ranks for some other ones to fill,
And now their mouldering bodies all lie on Shiloh Hill.

And now my song is ended, about those bloody plains,
I hope the sight by mortal man may ne'er be seen again;
But I pray to God, the Savior, "If consistent with Thy will,
To save the souls of all who fell on bloody Shiloh Hill."

The Battle Cry of Freedom

Three months after Shiloh, at a Union war rally in Chicago, a singing group called the Lumbard Brothers introduced the "Battle Cry of Freedom." The Hutchinson Family introduced the song in New York. It proved to be one of the greatest marching songs of the war, and remained a morale booster for Union troops throughout the war.

The Battle Cry of Freedom

Words and music: George Frederick Root.

Yes, we'll rally 'round the flag, boys, we'll rally once again,
Shouting the battle cry of Freedom,
We will rally from the hillside, we'll gather from the plain,
Shouting the battle cry of Freedom.

CHORUS
The Union forever, Hurrah boys, hurrah!
Down with the Traitor, up with the Star;
Yes, we'll rally 'round the flag, boys, we'll rally once again,
Shouting the battle cry of Freedom.

We are springing to the call for Three Hundred Thousand more,
Shouting the battle cry of freedom,
And we'll fill the vacant ranks of our brothers gone before,
Shouting the battle cry of freedom.

We will welcome to our numbers the loyal true and brave,
Shouting the battle cry of Freedom,
And although he may be poor he shall never be a slave,
Shouting the battle cry of Freedom.

So we're springing to the call from the East and from the West,
Shouting the battle cry of Freedom,
And we'll hurl the rebel crew from the land we love the best,
Shouting the battle cry of Freedom.

The Southern Battle Cry of Freedom

In self-defense Southerners wrote their own version, called "The Southern Battle Cry of Freedom."

The Southern Battle Cry of Freedom

Words: W. H. Barnes. Music: George Frederick Root.

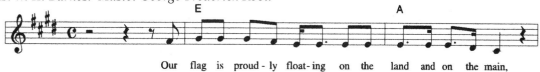

Our flag is proud-ly float-ing on the land and on the main,

Shout, shout, the bat-tle cry of Free-dom; Be-neath it oft we've con-quered and will

con-quer oft a-gain, Shout, shout, the bat-tle cry of Free-dom. Our

Dix-ie for-e-ver, she's ne-ver at a loss, Down with the ea-gle and

up with the cross, And we'll ral-ly 'round the bon-ny flag, we'll ral-ly once a-gain,

Shout, shout the bat-tle cry of Free-dom.

Our flag is proudly floating on the land and on the main,
Shout, shout, the battle cry of Freedom;
Beneath it oft we've conquered and will conquer oft again,
Shout, shout, the battle cry of Freedom.

CHORUS
Our Dixie forever, she's never at a loss,
Down with the eagle and up with the cross,
And we'll rally 'round the bonny flag, we'll rally once again,
Shout, shout, the battle cry of Freedom.

Our gallant boys have marched to the rolling of the drums,
Shout, shout, the battle cry of Freedom;
And the leaders in charge cry, "Come, boys, come!"
Shout, shout, the battle cry of Freedom.

They have laid down their lives on the bloody battle field,
Shout, shout, the battle cry of Freedom;
Their motto is resistance - "To tyrants we'll not yield!"
Shout, shout, the battle cry of Freedom.

While our boys have responded and to the field have gone,
Shout, shout, the battle cry of Freedom;
Our noble women also have aided them at home,
Shout, shout, the battle cry of Freedom.

Northern soldiers also sang parodies of "The Battle Cry of Freedom," including the following:

Mary had a little lamb, 'twas always on the go.
Shouting the battle cry of freedom,
So she staked it on a grassy slope along the Shenando'
Shouting the battle cry of freedom.

CHORUS
Hurrah for Mary! Hurrah for the lamb!
Hurrah for the soldiers who didn't care a damn,
For we'll rally 'round the flag, boys, we'll rally once again,
Shouting the battle cry of freedom.

It swam across the Shenando', our pickets saw it too,
Shouting the battle cry of freedom,
And speedily it simmered down into a mutton stew,
Shouting the battle cry of freedom.

And Mary never more did see her darling little lamb,
Shouting the battle cry of freedom,
For the boys in Blue they chawed it up and didn't give a damn,
Shouting the battle cry of freedom.

Goober Peas

The war stimulated the Northern industrial economy. The increased production for the war effort raised wages and morale. On the other hand, the South's agrarian economy suffered. Cotton fields were left untilled, the naval blockade prevented trade, and civilian morale dropped. In an attempt to hold down inflation, the Confederate government paid less than market value for crops.

When the Southern army began seizing grain at less than half the market value, many farmers withheld their grain, and some stopped planting. The result was an acute food shortage for the Southern soldiers. They complained about their diet of peanuts, which they called "goober peas."

The term "goober" derives from the West African word "nguba," which means "peanuts." Georgia soldiers were sometimes referred to as "goober grabbers." "Goober Peas" was a popular Confederate camp song during the war, but was not published until after the war. The words were attributed to "P. Pindar, Esq.," and the music to "P. Nutt, Esq."

Goober Peas

Words and music: anonymous.

Sittin' by the roadside on a summer's day,
Chatting with my messmates, passing time away,
Lyin'in the shadow underneath the trees,
Goodness how delicious, eating goober peas.

CHORUS
Peas! peas! peas! peas! eating goober peas!
Goodness how delicious, eating goober peas!

When a horseman passes the soldiers have a rule,
To cry out at their loudest, "Hey, mister, here's your mule!"
But another pleasure enchantinger than these,
Is wearin' out your grinders eating goober peas!

Just before the battle the General hears a row,
He says "The Yanks are comin', I hear their rifles now."
He turns around in wonder, and what do you think he sees?
The Georgia Militia, eating goober peas!

I think my song has lasted almost long enough,
The subject's interesting, but rhymes are rather tough,
I wish this war was over when free from lice and fleas
We'd kiss our wives and sweethearts and gobble goober peas!

Hard Crackers Come Again No More

Complaints about the food, or lack of food, were not limited to the Confederate soldiers. The Yankees sang this song, a parody of Stephen Foster's "Hard Times Come Again No More."

Hard Crackers Come Again No More

Words: anonymous. Music: Stephen Foster.

There's a hungry, thirsty soldier who wears his life away,
With torn clothes, whose better days are o'er;
He is sighing now for whiskey, and with throat as dry as hay
Sings, "Hard crackers come again no more."

CHORUS
'Tis the song and the sigh of the hungry,
"Hard crackers, hard crackers, come again no more!
Many days you have lingered upon our stomachs sore,
Oh, hard crackers, come again no more."

Let us close our game of poker, take our tin cups in hand,
While we gather 'round the cook's tent door,
Where dry mummies of hard crackers are given to each man;
"Oh, hard crackers come again no more!"

'Tis the song that is uttered in camp by night and day,
'Tis the wail that is mingled with each snore;
'Tis the sighing of the soul for spring chickens far away,
"Oh, hard crackers come again no more."

Army Grub

The tune is "America" or "God Save the Queen."
The term "S.B." means "so bad!"

Army Grub

Words and music: anonymous.

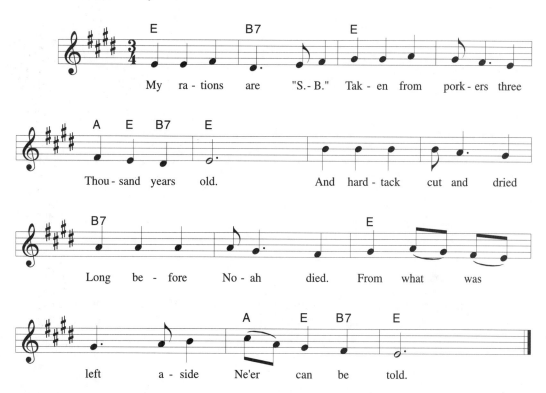

My ra - tions are "S.- B." Tak - en from pork - ers three
Thou - sand years old. And hard - tack cut and dried
Long be - fore No - ah died. From what was
left a - side Ne'er can be told.

Our rations are "S.B."
Taken from porkers three
Thousand years old.
And hardtack, cut and dried
Long before Noah died.
From what was left aside
Ne'er can be told.

The Army Bean/Army Bugs

Beans were the staple food, and bugs, especially lice, plagued the soldiers. Soldiers sang both songs to J. P. Webster's ever popular revival song "The Sweet Bye and Bye."

The Army Bean

Words: anonymous. Music: J. P. Webster.

There's a spot that the sol-diers all love. The mess tent is the place that we mean, And the dish we like best to see there Is the old-fash-ioned white ar-my bean 'Tis the bean that we mean, And we'll eat as we ne'er ate be-fore The ar-my bean nice and clean We will stick to our beans ev-er-more.

There's a spot that the soldiers all love.
The mess tent is the place that we mean,
And the dish we like best to see there
Is the old-fashioned white army bean.

CHORUS
'Tis the bean that we mean,
And we'll eat as we ne'er ate before;
The army bean, nice and clean,
We will stick to our beans ever more.

Now the bean in its primitive state
Is a plant we have all often met;
And when cooked in the old army style
It has charms we can never forget.

The German is fond of sauerkraut,
The potato is loved by the Mick,
But the soldiers have long since found out
That through life to our beans we should stick.

Army Bugs

Words: Anonymous. Music: J.P. Webster.

Sol-diers sing of their beans and can-teens, Of the cof-fee in the old ar-my cup, Why not men-tion the small friends we've seen Al-ways try-ing to chew ar-mies up? **Chorus** Those firm friends, tire-less friends, Hard-ly ev-er neg-lect-ing their hugs, Their re-gard, it nev-er ends, Oh how they loved us, those old ar-my bugs!

Soldiers sing of their beans and canteens,
Of the coffee in the old army cup,
Why not mention the small friends we've seen
Always trying to chew armies up?

CHORUS
Those firm friends, tireless friends,
Hardly ever neglecting their hugs,
Their regard, it never ends,
Oh how they loved us, those old army bugs!

The Homespun Dress

The food shortage also affected civilians. In April, 1863, women in Richmond staged a "bread riot" during which more that a thousand hungry women marched into bakeries, each one helping herself to a loaf of bread. They defied the Richmond City Battalion and marched home with the bread.

The South endured other shortages in addition to food. Wealthy women as well as poor learned to improvise. Nearly every woman learned to card, spin, knit, weave and crochet, in order to make clothing.

They braided palmetto to make hats, baskets and fans. They made shoes by knitting the tops and making soles out of home-tanned leather, made dyes from indigo weed, grew poppies for opium to make laudanum. They even learned to make a substitute for baking soda from the ashes of corn cobs. A favorite song that remained in oral tradition long after the war ended was "The Homespun Dress," sung to the tune of "The Bonnie Blue Flag."

The Homespun Dress

Words: Carrie Bell Sinclair. Music: anonymous.

Oh, yes I am a South-ern girl and glo-ry in the name, And boast it with far great-er pride than glit-t'ry wealth or fame. We en-vy not the North-ern girl, her robes of beau-ty rare, Though dia-monds grace her snow-y neck, and pearls be-deck her hair. Hur-rah! hur-rah! for the sun-ny South so dear, Three cheers for the home-spun dress the South-ern la-dies wear.

Oh, yes I am a Southern girl and glory in the name,
And boast it with far greater pride than glittering wealth or fame.
We envy not the Northern girl, her robes of beauty rare,
Though diamonds grace her snowy neck, and pearls bedeck her hair.

CHORUS
Hurrah! hurrah! for the sunny South so dear,
Three cheers for the homespun dress the Southern ladies wear.

The homespun dress is plain, I know, my hat's palmetto, too;
But then it shows what Southern girls for Southern rights will do.
We've sent the bravest of our land to battle with the foe,
And we will lend a helping hand, we love the South, you know.

The soldier is the lad for me, a brave heart I adore;
And when the sunny South is free and fighting is no more,
I'll choose me then a lover brave from out the gallant band,
The soldier lad I love the best shall have my heart and hand.

The Southern land's a glorious land, and has a glorious cause;
Then cheer three cheers for Southern rights and for the Southern boys.
We scorn to wear a bit of silk, a bit of Northern lace;
But make our homespun dresses up, and wear them with such grace.

Now, Northern goods are out of date, and since old Abe's blockade,
We Southern girls can be content with goods that's Southern made.
We sent our sweethearts to the war, but dear girls never mind,
Your soldier-love will ne'er forget the girl he left behind.

And now, young man, a word to you, if you would win the fair,
Go to the field where honor calls and win your lady there.
Remember that our brightest smiles are for the true and brave,
And that our tears are all for those who fill a soldier's grave.

We Are Coming, Father Abraham

Fierce independence, freedom and individualism characterized white Southerners. They cherished their states rights and their individual freedom, and even in wartime tolerated dissent. Soldiers often went home to their farms after a victorious battle. They elected their own officers, petitioned for the removal of officers, and sometimes even rode the officer on a rail until he agreed to behave himself. This exercise of individual freedom resulted in instability among the Confederate armed forces.

The Southern Conscription Act of April, 1862, was enacted to create a more stable army. Southerners strongly resented the act. Many soldiers deserted in protest, but the need for men outweighed the protests. The new conscription act retained existing volunteers after their term of service was over, and subjected Southern white men between the ages of 18 and 35 to the draft. In July, 1863, the draft age increased to 45, and by February, 1864, the Confederacy was drafting men aged 17 to 50.

The North needed men, too. On August 4, 1862, President Lincoln called for 300,000 volunteers. He did so with the warning that if the volunteers were not forthcoming, he would draft them from the militia. The response was overwhelming, 400,000 Northerners volunteered.

The New York "Evening Post" published the words to "We Are Coming, Father Abraham" in July, 1862, shortly after Lincoln's call for volunteers. At least eight composers, including Stephen Foster, wrote music to accompany the words, and the song was also sung to the Irish patriotic song "The Wearin' Of the Green." The version used here was published in 1862 by Oliver Ditson & Co. On the sheet music the publisher incorrectly attributed the words to William Cullen Bryant instead of James Gibbons.

We Are Coming, Father Abraham

Words: James Sloan Gibbons. Music: Luther Orland Emerson.

We are com - ing, Fa - ther A - bra'am, three hun - dred thou - sand more, From Mis - sis - sip - pi's wind - ing streams and from New Eng - land's shore; We leave our plows and work - shops, our wives and child - ren dear, With hearts too full for ut - ter - ance, with but a si - lent tear; We dare not look be - hind us, but stead - fast - ly be - fore, We are com - ing, Fa - ther A - bra'am - Three hun - dred thou - sand more! We are com - ing we are com - ing, our Un - ion to re - store; We are com - ing, Fa - ther

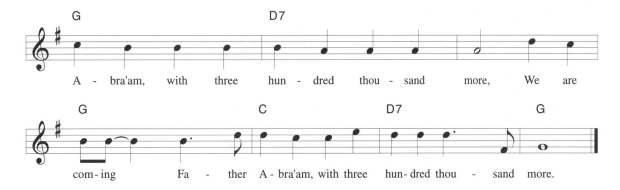

A - bra'am, with three hun - dred thou - sand more, We are
com - ing Fa - ther A - bra'am, with three hun - dred thou - sand more.

We are coming, Father Abra'am, three hundred thousand more,
From Mississippi's winding stream and from New England's shore;
We leave our plows and workshops, our wives and children dear,
With hearts too full for utterance, with but a silent tear;
We dare not look behind us, but steadfastly before,
We are coming Father Abra'am, three hundred thousand more!

CHORUS
We are coming, we are coming, our Union to restore;
We are coming Father Abra'am with three hundred thousand more,
We are coming Father Abra'am with three hundred thousand more.

If you look across the hill tops that meet the northern sky,
Long moving lines of rising dust your vision may descry;
And now the wind, an instant, tears the cloudy veil aside,
And floats aloft our spangled flag in glory and in pride;
And bayonets in the sunlight gleam, and bands brave music pour,
We are coming, Father Abra'am - three hundred thousand more!

If you look all up our valleys, where the growing harvests shine,
You may see our sturdy farmer boys fast forming into line;
And children from their mothers' knees are pulling at the weeds,
And learning how to reap and sow, against their country's needs;
And a farewell group stands weeping at every cottage door,
We are coming Father Abra'am - three hundred thousand more!

You have called us and we're coming, by Richmond's bloody tide,
To lay us down for freedom's sake, our brothers' bones beside;
Or from foul treason's savage group, to wrench the murderous blade,
And in the face of foreign foes its fragments to parade;
Six hundred thousand loyal men and true have gone before,
We are coming, Father Abra'am - three hundred thousand more!

Marketplace in Cincinnati

Come in out of the Draft

In 1863, the Union needed still more men, and Congress passed the Federal Conscription Act, covering men aged 20 to 45. The draft law had a provision that a man whose name was drawn could pay a commutation fee of $300 and be released from serving, until the next drawing, and he could be permanently released if he could provide a substitute.

"Come in out of the Draft" was published in 1863.

Charge of the police at the Tribune office

Come in out of the Draft

Words: Ednor Rossiter. Music: B. Frank Walthers.

As it was rath-er warm, I thought the oth-er day, I'd find some cool-er place the sum-mer months to stay; I had not long been gone when a pa-per to me came, And in the list of con-scripts I chanced to see my name. I showed it to my friends, and at me they all laughed. They said, "How are you con-script? Come in out of the draft."

As it was rather warm, I thought the other day,
I'd find some cooler place the summer months to stay;
I had not long been gone when a paper to me came,
And in the list of conscripts I chanced to see my name.
I showed it to my friends, and at me they all laughed,
They said, "How are you, conscript? Come in out of the draft."

Oh, soon I hurried home, for I felt rather blue;
I thought I'd ask my dad what I had better do;
Says he, "You are not young, you're over thirty-five;
The best thing you can do, sir, is go and take a bride."
My mother on me smiled, my brother at me laughed,
And said, "How are you, conscript? Come in out of the draft."

I soon made up my mind that I would take a wife;
For she could save my cash, and I could save my life.
I called upon a friend, I offered her my hand,
But she said she couldn't see it, for she loved some other man.
She told it to her man, and at me they both laughed,
And said, "How are you, conscript? Come in out of the draft."

So next I advertised, and soon a chap I found
Who said that he would go for just two hundred down.
I took him home to sleep. Says I, "Now I'm all right."
But, when I woke, I found that he'd robbed me in the night!
I went and told the mayor; the people 'round me laughed,
And said, "How are you, conscript? Come in out of the draft."

I to the provost went, my "notice" in my hand;
I found a crowd around, and with it took my stand.
I waited there till night, from early in the morn,
And, when I got inside, my pocket-book was gone!
I thought I should go mad! but everybody laughed,
And said, "How are you, conscript? Come in out of the draft."

I've tried to get a wife, I've tried to get a "sub,"
But what I next shall do, now really is the "rub."
My money's almost gone, and I am nearly daft;
Will some one tell me what to do to get out of the draft?
I've asked my friends all 'round, but at me they all laughed,
And said, "How are you, conscript? Come in out of the draft."

We Are Coming, Father Abraham, Three Hundred Dollars More

The $300 commutation fee was well beyond the economic range of working people, especially the foreign-born, and they complained that this was "a poor man's war." Two days after the first drawing of names for the draft in New York City, rioting broke out. The rioters, mostly Irish, burned and looted for three days. Officials estimated that 1,000 people were killed, and that rioters destroyed property worth a million and a half dollars.

We Are Coming, Father Abraham, Three Hundred Dollars More

Words: Tony Pastor. Music: Luther Orland Emerson.

We are coming, Father Abra'am, three hundred dollars more,
We're rich enough to stay at home, let them go out that's poor.
But Uncle Abe, we're not afraid to stay behind in clover,
We'll nobly fight, defend the right, when this cruel war is over.

For Bales

The Confederacy believed that cotton was the way to victory, that without Southern cotton the North would have to close their textile mills, causing severe economic hardship. They also believed that if they withheld cotton from Britain and France, those countries would be forced to come to the aid of the South.

The embargo backfired. Britain and France chose not to intervene. Smugglers and some Southern farmers traded cotton with the North. As Union troops moved South, the Confederate government was forced to destroy two and a half million bales of valuable cotton to prevent it from falling into Federal hands.

Union General Nathaniel Prentiss Banks was in command of the Red River campaign in Louisiana when Confederate Generals Richard Taylor and E. Kirby Smith thwarted his attempt to seize Southern cotton. This Confederate song was sung to "When Johnny Comes Marching Home."

Opening of the Mississippi – Arrival of the "Imperial" at New Orleans

For Bales

Words: A. E. Blackmar. Music: Patrick S. Gilmore.

We all went down to New Orleans for Bales, for Bales,
We all went down to New Orleans for Bales, says I,
We all went down to New Orleans to get a peek behind the scenes,
And we'll all drink stone blind, Johnny fill up the bowl.

We thought when we got in the "Ring," for Bales, for Bales,
We thought when we got in the "Ring" for Bales, says I,
We thought when we got in the "Ring," greenbacks would be a dead sure thing,
And we'll all drink stone blind, Johnny fill up the bowl.

The "Ring" went up, with bagging and rope, for Bales, for Bales,
Upon the "Black Hawk" with bagging and rope, for Bales, says I,
Went up "Red River" with bagging and rope, expecting to make a pile of "soap,"
And we'll all drink stone blind, Johnny fill up the bowl.

But Taylor and Smith, with ragged ranks, for Bales, for Bales,
But Taylor and Smith, with ragged ranks, for Bales, says I,
But Taylor and Smith, with ragged ranks, burned the cotton and whipped old Banks,
And we'll all drink stone blind, Johnny fill up the bowl.

Our "Ring" came back and cursed and swore, for Bales, for Bales,
Our "Ring" came back and cursed and swore, for Bales, says I,
Our "Ring" came back and cursed and swore, for we got no cotton at Grand Ecore,
And we'll all drink stone blind, Johnny fill up the bowl.

Now let us all give praise and thanks for Bales, for Bales,
Now let us all give praise and thanks for Bales, says I,
Now let us all give praise and thanks for the victory (?) gained by General Banks,
And we'll all drink stone blind, Johnny fill up the bowl.

The Changing War

The United States sloop of war "Brooklyn"

Kingdom Coming

When the war began, African-Americans on both sides of the Mason-Dixon line responded. Many offers to serve the Confederacy came from Virginia's 60,000 free blacks. Most of their labors went toward building defenses and fortifications for the cities.

In Norfolk, the Petersburg Express said:

"The entire fortifications of the harbor might be constructed by the voluntary labors of negroes, who would claim no higher reward than the privilege of being allowed to contribute their share toward the defense of the state..."

Many body servants and household slaves remained faithful to their Southern masters throughout the war, and many field hands remained on the plantations. They produced the crops that fed the Confederate army. The army impressed skilled black workers into non-combat service.

While many slaves remained loyal to their masters, the majority did not. Their attitudes were summed up in a tongue-in-cheek advertisement which a slave in Beaufort, South Carolina, posted for the return of his runaway master:

"$500 reward. Ran away from me on the 7th of this month, my master Julian Rhett. Master Rhett is five feet eleven inches high, big shoulders, black hair, curly shaggy whiskers, low forehead, and dark face. He makes a big fuss when he goes among the gentlemen, he talks very big, and uses the name of the Lord all the time. Calls himself "Southern Gentleman." Master Rhett has a deep scar on his shoulder from a fight, a scratch across the left eye, made by my Dinah when he tried to whip her. He never looks people in the face. I more than expect he will make tracks for Bergen County, in the foreign land of Jersey, where I imagine he has a few friends.

I will give four hundred dollars for him if alive, and five hundred if anybody will show him dead. If he comes back to his kind Niggers without much trouble, this child will receive him lovingly."

The Christy Minstrels introduced "Kingdom Coming" in Chicago in April, 1862. The words were written in dialect, portraying the enjoyment of slaves watching their master retreating before the Union army. Despite the sentiments, the song was popular in the South as well as the North, and still survives in oral tradition.

Legend has it that the conquering black troops sang "Kingdom Coming" as they entered Richmond, Virginia.

Kingdom Coming

Words and music: Henry Clay Work.

Say, dar-keys hab you seen de mas-sa, wid de muff-stash on his face, Go 'long de road some time dis morn-in' like he gwine to leab de place? He see a smoke, way up de rib-ber whar de Lin-kum gum-boats lay; He took his hat an' lef ber-ry sud-den, an' I spec he's run a-

way! De mas - sa run? Ha, ha! De dark - ey stay? Ho,

ho! It mus' be now de king-dom com-in' an' de year of Ju - bi - lo!

Say, darkeys hab you seen de massa, wid de muffstash on his face,
Go long de road some time dis mornin' like he gwine to leab de place?
He see a smoke, way up ribber whar de Linkum gumboats lay;
He took his hat an' lef berry sudden, an' I spec he's run away!

CHORUS
De massa run? ha! ha! De darkey stay? ho! ho!
It mus' be now de kingdom comin' an' de year of Jubilo!

He's six foot one way, two feet tudder, an' he weigh tree hundred pound,
His coat so big, he couldn't pay de tailor, an' it won't go half way round.
He drill so much day call him Cap'an, an' he get so dreful tann'd,
I spec he try an' fool dem Yankees for to tink he's contraband.

De darkeys feel so lonesome libing in de log house on de lawn,
Dey move dar tings to massa's parlor for to keep it while he's gone.
Dar's wine an' cider in de kitchen, an' de darkeys dey'll hab some;
I spose day'll all be cornfiscated when de Linkum sojers come.

De oberseer he make us trouble, an' he dribe us round a spell;
We lock him up in de smokehouse cellar,
wid de key trown in de well.
De whip is lost, de han'cuff broken, but de massa'll hab his pay;
He's ole enough, big enough,
ought to known better dan to went an' run away.

Benjamin F. Butler

No More Auction Block for Me

On May 23, 1861, three runaway slaves entered Fortress Monroe in Virginia, and surrendered themselves to the Union army. General Benjamin F. Butler, an attorney, determined that they were "contraband of war," and therefore refused to return them to their owners. Thanks to General Butler, escaped slaves came to be known as "contrabands."

News of Butler's decision spread quickly throughout the slave underground. Within three days, slaves valued at $60,000 had entered the fortress. In the next four months, 15,000 African-Americans escaped to the Union military forces.

In his book Army Life in a Black Regiment, Colonel Thomas Wentworth Higginson quotes the words to this song, sung by his African-American troops who served in the First South Carolina Volunteer Regiment. Higginson says the peck of corn and pint of salt referred to in the song were slave rations. The tune is from the Ashanti.

No More Auction Block for Me

Words and music: anonymous.

No more auc - tion block for me, no more, no more, no more. No more auc - tion block for me, man - y thou - sand gone.

No more auction block for me, no more, no more,
No more auction block for me, many thousand gone.

No more peck of corn for me, no more, no more,
No more peck of corn for me, many thousand gone.

No more pint of salt for me, no more, no more,
No more pint of salt for me, many thousand gone.

No more driver's lash for me, no more, no more,
No more driver's lash for me, many thousand gone.

Slavery Chain Done Broke at Last

Some Union commanders refused sanctuary to runaways, and sent them back to their masters. Others, like General John C. Frémont and "Black Dave" Hunter, set them free.

The contrabands supplied Northern Generals with up-to-date information on Confederate positions and fortifications. Many became guides for the Union army.

The navy, too, received help from the contrabands, learning of the locations of Confederate ships. In one instance, ten Union mortar-vessels were saved from capture through information received from runaway slaves.

The melody is African-American, from the song "Joshua Fit the Battle of Jericho."

Slavery Chain Done Broke at Last

Words and music: anonymous.

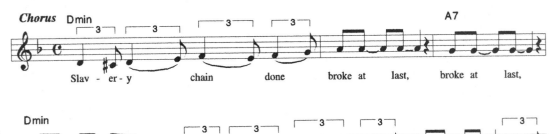

CHORUS
Slavery chain done broke at last, broke at last, broke at last,
Slavery chain done broke at last, gonna praise God 'til I die.

Way up in that valley, just prayin' on my knees,
Telling God all about my troubles, yes, and to help me if He please.

Well I told Him how I suffered in the dungeon and the chain,
And the days I went with head bowed down and my broken flesh and pain.

Well I know my Jesus heard me, 'cause the Spirit spoke to me,
Said, "Rise up now my servant, and you too shall be free."

There's no more weary travelin', 'cause my Jesus set me free,
And there's no more auction block since He gave me Liberty.

Oh, Freedom

At the beginning of the war, African-Americans were not allowed to bear arms in the Union army. But by mid-1862, General David Hunter had organized the first black regiment to serve the North. It was called the First South Carolina Volunteer Regiment, and was made up of contrabands from South Carolina and Florida.

In the South, black soldiers were not recruited until the end of the war. The one exception was in New Orleans, where, ironically, the same black soldiers served both the Confederacy and the Union.

When Admiral Farragut captured New Orleans, the Confederate army retreated, leaving behind two regiments made up of free blacks. In August, 1862, General Butler asked them to serve in the Union army. They agreed, and were mustered into the United States army as The Louisiana Native Guards.

"Oh Freedom" became the marching song of the African-American regiments during the Civil War.

Oh, Freedom

Words and music: anonymous.

Oh, Freedom, Oh, Freedom, Oh, Freedom after a while,
And before I'd be a slave, I'd be buried in my grave,
And go home to my Lord, and be free.

No more moaning, no more moaning, no more moaning after a while,
And before I'd be a slave, I'd be buried in my grave,
And go home to my Lord, and be free.

There'll be shoutin', there'll be shoutin', there'll be shoutin' after a while,
And before I'd be a slave, I'd be buried in my grave,
And go home to my Lord, and be free.

Oh, Freedom, Oh, Freedom, Oh, Freedom, after a while,
And before I'd be a slave, I'd be buried in my grave,
And go home to my Lord, and be free.

Go Down Moses

The problem of slavery plagued the Union. In the beginning, Lincoln opposed slavery, but had no intention of breaking United States laws to abolish it.

He had two plans:

The first was to have the government buy slaves from the slave-owners in those states still in the Union. Congress began the process by passing the District of Columbia Emancipation Act, abolishing slavery in Washington, D.C., and paying up to $300 for each person freed.

The second plan was to colonize African-Americans outside the limits of the United States. Congress appropriated twenty million dollars for this purpose.

"Outside the United States" meant Haiti, Liberia or, Lincoln's preference, the Chiriqui province, a two million acre land grant located in present-day Panama.

Lincoln's plans met with two major obstacles: slaveholders in the Union refused to sell their slaves to the government, and most free blacks refused to leave the country. In August, 1862, Robert Purvis sent the following message to the government emigration agent:

"The children of the black man have enriched the soil by their tears, and sweat, and blood. Sir, we were born here, and here we choose to remain."

In the meantime, slaves continued to escape to the North. Harriet Tubman, who had been a slave, helped hundreds of her fellow African-Americans escape from slavery. Her code name was "Moses," and she is said to be the Moses referred to in the song.

Go Down Moses

Words and music: anonymous.

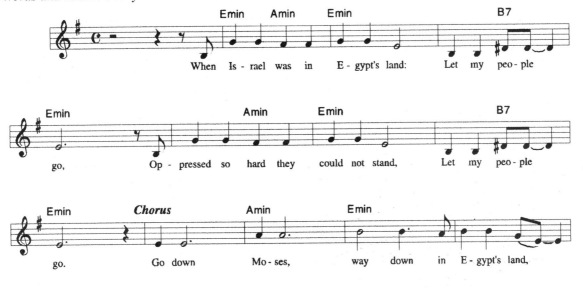

When Israel was in Egypt's land: let my people go,
Oppressed so hard they could not stand, let my people go.

CHORUS
Go down, Moses, way down in Egypt land,
Tell old Pharaoh, let my people go.

Thus saith the Lord, bold Moses said, let my people go;
If not I'll smite your first-born dead, let my people go.

No more shall they in bondage toil, let my people go;
Let them come out with Egypt's spoil, let my people go.

When Israel out of Egypt came, let my people go;
And left the proud oppressive land, let my people go.

O 'twas a dark and dismal night, let my people go;
When Moses led the Israelites, let my people go.

'Twas good old Moses and Aaron, too, let my people go;
'Twas they that led the armies through, let my people go.

The Lord told Moses what to do. Let my people go;
To lead the children of Israel through, let my people go.

continued on the next page

O come along, Moses, you'll not get lost, let my people go;
Stretch out your rod and come across, let my people go.

As Israel stood by the water side, let my people go;
At the command of God it did divide, let my people go.

When they had reached the other shore, let my people go;
They sang a song of triumph o'er, let my people go.

Pharaoh said he would go across, let my people go;
But Pharaoh and his host were lost, let my people go.

O, Moses, the cloud shall cleave the way, let my people go;
A fire by night, a shade by day, let my people go.

You'll not get lost in the wilderness, let my people go;
With a lighted candle in your breast, let my people go.

Jordan shall stand up like a wall, let my people go;
And the walls of Jericho shall fall, let my people go.

Your foes shall not before you stand, let my people go;
And you'll possess fair Canaan's land, let my people go.

'Twas just about in harvest time, let my people go;
When Joshua led his host divine, let my people go.

O let us all from bondage flee, let my people go;
And let us all in Christ be free, let my people go.

We need not always weep and moan, let my people go;
And wear these slavery chains forlorn, let my people go.

This world's a wilderness of woe, let my people go;
O, let us on to Canaan go, let my people go.

What a beautiful morning that will be, let my people go;
When time breaks up in eternity, let my people go.

O brethren, brethren, you'd better be engaged, let my people go;
For the Devil he's out on a big rampage, let my people go.

The Devil he thought he had me fast, let my people go;
But I thought I'd break his chains at last, let my people go.

O take your shoes from off your feet, let my people go;
And walk into the golden street, let my people go.

I'll tell you what I like the best, let my people go;
It is the shouting Methodist, let my people go.

I do believe without a doubt, let my people go;
That a Christian has the right to shout, let my people go.

Free at Last

Lincoln pushed hard for emigration in the summer of 1862, because he had decided to issue a proclamation freeing the slaves. He felt emancipation would be accepted more readily by Northern whites if the freed slaves created a separate nation.

In September, Lincoln issued a warning that slaves in states still in rebellion on January first would be free forever.

True to his word, on January 1, 1863, Abraham Lincoln issued the Emancipation Proclamation. The War to Preserve the Union had now become a Holy War for Freedom.

Free at Last

Words and music: anonymous.

CHORUS
Free at last, free at last, I thank God I'm free at last;
Free at last, free at last, I thank God I'm free at last.

Way down yonder in the graveyard walk, I thank God I'm free at last,
Me and my Jesus gonna meet and talk, I thank God I'm free at last.

On my knees when the light passed by, I thank God I'm free at last;
I thought my soul would rise and fly, I thank God I'm free at last.

Some of these mornings, bright and fair, I thank God I'm free at last;
Gonna meet my Jesus in the middle of the air, I thank God I'm free at last.

LAST CHORUS
Free at last, free at last, I thank God I'm free at last;
Free at last, free at last, thank God Almighty I'm free at last!

One hundred years after the Civil War, 200,000 black and white Americans peacefully marched on Washington, D.C., expressing their demands for civil rights. When the Reverend Martin Luther King, Jr. addressed the crowd, he quoted from this song, and the words were later inscribed on his headstone.

John Brown's Body

The Emancipation Proclamation included a provision that freed slaves would be "received into the armed service of the United States, to garrison forts, positions, stations and other places and to man vessels of all sorts in said service."

Massachusetts Governor John Andrews received authorization to raise a regiment of African-American volunteers. He advertised widely. With the help of recruiting agents, including Frederick Douglass, 1,000 volunteers from every state in the Union and from Canada were organized to become the Massachusetts Fifty-Fourth. On May 28, 1863, the 54th paraded through Boston, with 20,000 citizens watching. As they marched, they sang "John Brown's Body."

Stories of the origins of "John Brown's Body" are numerous and varied. One story has it originating spontaneously from a parade in Boston shortly after word arrived that John Brown had been hanged at Harper's Ferry. Another claims that the four sergeants in the Boston Light Infantry Quartet improvised some words about Sergeant John Brown, one of the quartet members. They sang the words to the tune of the old camp meeting song "Say Brothers Will You Meet Us?"

"John Brown's Body" is often referred to as the "emancipation Marseillaise," and enjoyed tremendous popularity among both black and white Union soldiers.

John Brown's Body

Words and music: anonymous.

John Brown's body lies a-mouldring in the grave,
John Brown's body lies a-mouldring in the grave,
John Brown's body lies a-mouldring in the grave,
His soul is marching on.

CHORUS
Glory, glory Hallelujah, glory, glory Hallelujah,
Glory, glory Hallelujah, his soul is marching on.

He captured Harper's Ferry with his nineteen men so true,
They frightened Old Virginny till she trembled through and through,
They hung him for a traitor, they themselves the traitor crew,
But his truth is marching on.

He's gone to be a soldier in the army of the Lord,
He's gone to be a soldier in the army of the Lord,
He's gone to be a soldier in the army of the Lord,
His soul is marching on.

John Brown died that the slave might be free,
John Brown died that the slave might be free,
John Brown died that the slave might be free,
But his soul is marching on.

Now has come the glorious jubilee,
Now has come the glorious jubilee,
Now has come the glorious jubilee,
When all mankind is free.

John Brown

The Marching Song of the First Arkansas Regiment

The valor of the Massachusetts Fifty-Fourth during their bloody assault on Fort Wagner in July, 1863, left no doubt that black troops would fight. They opened the way for the rest of the 180,000 African-American troops who fought in 500 battles and suffered 60,000 deaths, a higher percentage than that suffered by white soldiers.

"The Marching Song of the First Arkansas Regiment," written by their white officer Captain Lindley Miller, was sung by the black troops who comprised the "First Arkansas," and was later published as a broadside to help recruit African-Americans into the Union army.

The Marching Song of the First Arkansas Regiment

Words: Captain Lindley Miller. Music: anonymous.

Oh we're the bully soldiers of the First of Arkansas,
We are fighting for the Union, we are fighting for the law,
We can shoot a Rebel further that a white man ever saw,
As we go marching on.

CHORUS
Glory, glory hallelujah,
Glory, glory hallelujah,
Glory, glory hallelujah,
As we go marching on.

They said "Now, colored brethren, you can be forever free,
From the first of January eighteen hundred sixty-three."
We heard it in the river going rushing to the sea
As it goes sounding on.

Father Abraham has spoken and the message has been sent.
The prison doors he opened, and out the prisoners went
To join the sable army of the African descent,
As we go marching on.

See, there above the center, where the flag is waving bright,
We are going out of slavery; we're bound for freedom's light;
We mean to show Jeff Davis how the Africans can fight,
As we go marching on!

They will have to pay us wages, the wages of their sin,
They will have to bow their foreheads to their colored kith and kin,
They will have to give us house-room, or the roof shall tumble in!
As we go marching on.

Then fall in, colored brethren, you'd better do it soon,
Don't you hear the drum a-beating the Yankee Doodle tune?
We are with you now this morning, we'll be far away at noon,
As we go marching on.

We heard the Proclamation, master hush it as he will,
The bird he sung it to us, hopping on the cotton hill,
And the possum up the gum tree, he couldn't keep it still,
As he went climbing on.

In addition to the black soldiers, nearly a quarter of a million African-American civilians served the Union army. They worked as teamsters, servants, cooks, laborers, wheelwrights, blacksmiths, foragers, spies, wagon masters, carpenters and masons. They built roads, bridges and fortifications.

Black women served as scouts, and many served as nurses. These volunteers included such famous names as Harriet Tubman, Susie King Taylor and Sojourner Truth. Sojourner Truth, then in her seventies, often brought gifts to the soldiers she was nursing, paying for them from money raised by lecturing and singing. She often sang:

We have done with raising cotton,
We have done with hoeing corn,
We are colored Yankee soldiers now,
As sure as you are born.
When the masters hear us yelling
They will think it's Gabriel's horn!
As we go marching on.

Negro Quarters Army of the James

The *Cumberland* and the *Merrimac*

In contrast to the army, the Union navy had never barred blacks from service. Prior to the war, African-Americans had made up about five per cent of the enlistments. The mess hall was integrated - black and white sailors worked well together. As escaped slaves flocked to the ships, the navy enlisted them for service under the same terms as any other enlistments.

Nearly 30,000 African-Americans served in the Union navy. By the end of the war, one out of every four Union sailors was black, and every Union ship had black crewmen.

The Civil War wrote a new chapter in naval warfare - the ironclads. The Confederates raised the sunken ship *Merrimac*, turned her into an ironclad, and renamed her the *Virginia*. She was slow and cumbersome, but deadly in her encounters with Federal warships. The first Union wooden sailing ship to battle the ironclad *Virginia* was the *Cumberland*. Heavy firepower from the *Cumberland* did very little damage to the *Virginia*, and she sent the *Cumberland* to the bottom. Only a third of the *Cumberland*'s crew of 346 men survived. The long era of the wooden warship was over.

The *Cumberland* and the *Merrimac*

Words and music: anonymous.

It was on last Monday morning, just at the break of day,
When the good ship called the *Cumberland* lay anchored in her way,
And the man upon our lookout to those below did say,
"I see something like a house top, on our leeward she does lay."

Our captain seized his telescope and he gazed far o'er the blue,
And then he turned and spoke to his brave and loyal crew,
"That thing which yonder lies floating, that looks like some turtle's back,
It's that infernal Rebel steamer, and they call her *Merrimac*."

Our decks were cleared for action and our guns were pointed through,
But still she kept a-coming up across the water blue,
And on, still on, she kept coming, till no distance stood apart;
When she sent a ball a-humming, stilled the beat of many a heart.

It was then we fired our broadside into her ribs of steel,
And yet no break in her iron made, no damage did she feel,
Till at length that Rebel pirate unto our captain spoke,
Saying, "Haul down your flying colors now,
or I'll sink your Yankee boat."

Our captain's eyes did glisten and his cheeks turned pale with rage,
And then in tones of thunder, to the Rebel pirate said:
"My men are brave and loyal, too, they're true to every man,
And before I'll strike my colors down, you may sink me in the sand."

Well, the *Merrimac* she left us then for a hundred yards or more,
Then with her whistles screaming out, on our wooden side she bore;
She struck us at our midship, and her ram went crashing through,
And the water came a-pouring in on our brave and loyal crew.

Well, our captain turned unto his men and unto them he did say,
"I'll never strike my colors down while the *Cumberland* rides the wave,
But I'll go down with my gallant ship for to meet a watery grave,
And you, my loyal comrades, you may seek your lives to save."

They swore they never would leave him,
but would man their guns afresh,
Poured broadside after broadside, till the water reached their breasts;
And then they sank far down, far down into the watery deep,
The Stars and Stripes still flying from her mainmast's highest peak.

The Virginia

The day after the sinking of the *Cumberland*, a Union ironclad called the *Monitor* steamed into the James River to challenge the *Virginia*. Firing at close range, it was obvious that neither ship could hurt the other, and the fight ended in a draw. The *Monitor* was so weighed down with armor that her flat deck sat just above the water. She was equipped with a revolving turret. The Confederates called her "a Yankee cheese box on a raft." The Union sailors responded to this description, singing:

A Yankee cheese box on a raft, they named our little boat,
I'm sure no better box of cheese was ever set afloat,
For catching rats we bait with cheese, for rebels do the same;
And if they'll only take the bait we'll surely catch our game.

Another song about the incident was "The *Cumberland* Crew." The final verse says:

Slowly she sank in the dark rolling waters,
Their voices on earth will ne'er be heard any more;
They'll be wept by Columbia's brave sons and fair daughters,
May their blood be avenged on Virginia's old shore:
And if ever our Sailors in battle assemble,
God bless our dear banner - "The Red, White and Blue!"
Beneath its proud folds we'll cause tyrants to tremble,
Or "Sink at our guns" like the Cumberland's *crew.*

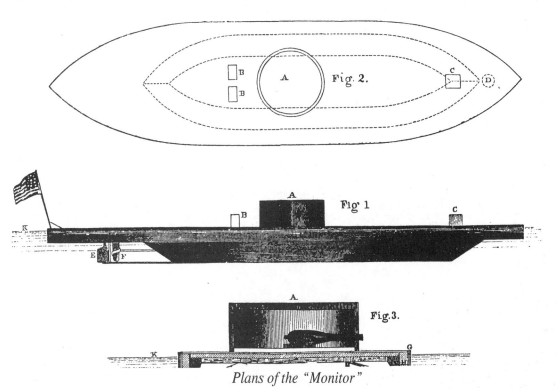

Plans of the "Monitor"

The *Alabama*

The scourge of the seas, however, was not an ironclad. It was a Confederate cruiser built in Liverpool, England, called the *Alabama*. During her two year career, the *Alabama* captured or destroyed more than eighty Union merchant vessels.

The *Alabama*

Words: E. King. Music: F. W. Rosier.

The wind blows off yon rock - y shore, boys, set your sails all free; And soon our boom - ing can - nons' roar shall ring out mer - ri - ly. Run up your bunt - ing taut a - peak and swear lads to de - fend her; 'Gainst ev - 'ry foe, where e're we go, our mot - to, "No sur - ren - der." Then sling the bowl, drink ev - 'ry soul, a toast to the Al - a - bam - a; - What - e're - our lot, through storm or shot, here's suc -

cess   to   the   Al - a - bam -   a!

The wind blows off yon rocky shore, boys, set your sails all free;
And soon our booming cannons' roar shall ring out merrily.
Run up your bunting taut a-peak, and swear, lads, to defend her;
'Gainst every foe, where'er we go, our motto, "No Surrender."

CHORUS
Then sling the bowl, drink every soul, a toast to the *Alabama*;
Whate'er our lot, through storm or shot, here's success to the *Alabama*!

Our country calls all hands to arms, we hear but to obey;
Nor shall home's most endearing charms steal one weak thought away.
Our saucy craft shall roam the deep, we've sworn, lads, to defend her;
Trim, taut and tight, we'll brave the fight, our motto, "No Surrender!"

Our home is on the mountain wave, our flag floats proudly free;
No boasting despot, tyrant, knave, shall crush fair Liberty.
Firmly we'll aid her glorious cause, we'll die, boys, to defend her;
We'll brave the foe where'er we go, our motto, "No Surrender!"

Boys, if perchance it may befall, when storm of battle raves,
By shot or shell our noble hull shall sink beneath the waves,
Yet while a plank to us is left, to death we will defend her;
Facing the foe, down, down we'll go, but still cry, "No Surrender!"

The *Alabama* was finally sunk by the
U.S.S Kearsarge. Northerners sang,
with a grudging respect for the
Alabama:

The Alabama*'s gone, hurrah!*
to Davy Jones's Locker far,
There's nothing left of her
to mar our commerce on the sea!

The Alabama

Kentucky, Oh Kentucky

Confederate guerillas were another thorn in the side of the Union, especially in Kansas, Missouri, Kentucky and Tennessee. Guerilla leaders in Kansas and Missouri included Cole Younger and William Clarke Quantrill, considered heroes by the Confederates, and labeled "bandits, bushwhackers and merciless fiends" by the Federals.

General John Morgan was the most celebrated of the Confederate guerilla leaders. Kentucky and Tennessee were terrorized by Morgan's Raiders. Morgan captured towns, cities, arms and other military equipment, burned bridges and destroyed government depots filled with provisions.

The tune is "Maryland, My Maryland."

Kentucky, Oh Kentucky

Words and music: anonymous.

John Mor-gan is foot is on thy shore, Ken-tuck-y, oh, Ken-tuck-y. His hand is on thy sta-ble door, Ken-tuck-y, oh, Ken-tuck-y. You'll see your good gray mare no more, he'll ride her till her back is sore, And leave her at some stran-ger's door, Ken-tuck-y, oh, Ken-tuck-y.

Morgan's Raiders

John Morgan's foot is on thy shore, Kentucky, oh, Kentucky.
His hand is on thy stable door, Kentucky, oh, Kentucky.
You'll see your good gray mare no more,
he'll ride her till her back is sore,
And leave her at some stranger's door, Kentucky, oh, Kentucky.

For feeding John, you're paying dear, Kentucky, oh, Kentucky.
His very name now makes you fear, Kentucky, oh, Kentucky.
In every valley far and near he's gobbled every horse and steer,
You'll rue his raids for many a year, Kentucky, oh, Kentucky.

Yet you have many a traitorous fool, Kentucky, oh, Kentucky.
Who still will be the Rebel's tool, Kentucky, oh, Kentucky.
They'll learn to yield to Abra'am's rule
in none but Johnny's costly school,
At cost of every "animule," Kentucky, oh, Kentucky.

How Are You, John Morgan?

After his capture in 1863, General John Morgan effected a spectacular escape, tunneling out from his prison cell. "How Are You, John Morgan?" sung to the tune of C. D. Benson's "Here's Your Mule," describes his escape.

How Are You, John Morgan?

Words: anonymous. Music: C. D. Benson.

A famous Rebel once was caught with sabre bright in hand,
Upon a mule he never bought, but pressed in Abram's land.
The Yankees caught his whole command in the great Ohio state;
And kept the leader of the band, to exchange for Colonel Streight.

CHORUS
Then raise the shout, the glorious shout, John Morgan's caught at last,
Proclaim it loud, the land throughout, he's into prison cast.

continued on next page

A felon's cell was then prepared at David Tod's request,
And in Columbus prison shared the convict's shaven crest.
And thus the Rebel chieftain's pride they sought to humble low,
But Southern valor don't subside nor less in prisons grow.

But prison fare he did not like, and sought a time to leave,
And with greenbacks and pocket knife, the keepers he did deceive.
They say he dug a tunnel 'neath its grated walls so grand,
And from the North he took "French leave" away for Dixie's land.

John Morgan's gone like lightning flies through every state and town;
Keep watch, and for the famous prize, five thousand dollars down.
But he is gone, too late, too late, his whereabouts to find,
He's gone to call on Master Jeff way down in Richmond town.

LAST CHORUS
Upon his mule, he's gone they say, to Dixie's promised land,
And at no very distant day to lead a new command.

John Morgan

Tramp! Tramp! Tramp!

The Confederate prison camp at Andersonville, Georgia, had no shelter for the prisoners, and no trees or other materials available to make shelters. No soap or clothing was issued. Southern captors gave their Northern prisoners raw food with no fuel and no utensils for cooking. Each day, between twenty and one hundred twenty Union soldiers died at Andersonville from disease and starvation.

Confederate soldiers encountered similar conditions in Northern prison camps, especially at Elmira, New York, and Camp Douglas, near Chicago. Twenty-six thousand Confederate soldiers died in Northern prisons, and thirty thousand Union soldiers died in Southern prisons.

George Root's "Tramp, Tramp, Tramp (The Prisoner's Hope)" became a favorite marching song among Union soldiers.

Interior view of the prison pen at Millen

Tramp! Tramp! Tramp!

Words and music: George Frederick Root.

In the prison cell I sit, thinking Mother dear, of you,
And our bright and happy home so far away,
And the tears they fill my eyes spite of all that I can do,
Though I try to cheer my comrades and be gay.

CHORUS
Tramp, tramp, tramp, the boys are marching,
Cheer up comrades they will come,
And beneath the starry flag we will breathe the air again,
Of the freeland in our own beloved home.

In the battle front we stood when their fiercest charge they made,
And they swept us off a hundred men or more,
But before we reached their lines they were beaten back dismayed
And we heard the cry of victory o'er and o'er.

So within the prison cell we are waiting for the day
That shall come to open wide the iron door,
And the hollow eye grows bright, and the poor heart almost gay,
As we think of seeing home and friends once more.

The Bonnie White Flag

Colonel Hawkins' song was printed in a prison camp newspaper in 1864, when Confederate hopes for victory were fading.

The Bonnie White Flag

Words: Colonel W. S. Hawkins. Music: anonymous.

Though we're a band of pris-on-ers, let each be firm and true, For no-ble souls and hearts of oak the foe can ne'er sub-due. We then will turn us home-ward to those we love so dear; For peace and hap-pi-ness, my boys, give a heart-y cheer! *Chorus* Hur-rah! Hur-rah! for peace and home, hur-rah! Hur-rah for the Bon-nie White Flag that ends this cru-el war!

Though we're a band of prisoners, let each be firm and true,
For noble souls and hearts of oak the foe can ne'er subdue.
We then will turn us homeward to those we love so dear;
For peace and happiness, my boys, give a hearty cheer!

CHORUS
Hurrah! Hurrah! for peace and home, hurrah!
Hurrah for the Bonnie White Flag that ends this cruel war!

The sword into the scabbard, the musket on the wall,
The cannon from its blazing throat no more shall hurl the ball;
From wives and babes and sweethearts, no longer will we roam,
For every gallant soldier boy shall seek his cherished home.

Our battle banners furled away no more shall greet the eye,
Nor beat of angry drums be heard, nor bugle's hostile cry.
The blade no more be raised aloft in conflict fierce and wild,
The bomb shall roll across the sward, the plaything of a child.

No pale-faced captive then shall stand behind his rusted bars;
Nor from the prison window bleak look sadly to the stars;
But out amid the woodland's green, on pounding steed he'll be,
And proudly from his heart shall rise the anthem of the free.

The plow into the furrow then, the fields shall wave with grain,
And smiling children to their schools all gladly go again.
The church invites its grateful throng, and man's rude striving cease,
While all across our noble land shall glow the light of peace.

Both Colonel Hawkins' "Bonnie White Flag" and George Root's "Tramp, Tramp, Tramp" lack the bitterness that many of the prison songs reflected. Northern prisoners at Libby Prison in Richmond, Virginia, defied their guards and roared out this song:

Oh, may that cuss, Jeff Davis float,
Glory Hallelujah!
On stormy sea, in open boat, in Iceland's cold, without a coat,
Glory Hallelujah!
While little devils dance in glee and lock the door and lose the key,
Glory Hallelujah!
And 'mid his roars and frantic cries,
Glory Hallelujah!
Oh, make eternal ashes rise, and blow forever in his eyes,
Glory Hallelujah!

Confederate prisoners being conducted from Jonesborough to Atlanta

When Johnny Comes Marching Home

As the war dragged on, civilians began to think more about the soldiers coming home than about victory and glory. Union army bandmaster Patrick Gilmore capitalized on these feelings when he published "When Johnny Comes Marching Home" in 1863. The original sheet music attributed authorship to Louis Lambert, a pen name used by the Irish-born Gilmore.

There has been some debate as to whether Gilmore actually composed the music. Some claim the tune to be Irish, others believe it to be an African-American melody. Whatever the source, "When Johnny Comes Marching Home" became one of America's all-time favorite tunes. Its popularity continued to grow after the Civil War, and reached its peak during the Spanish American War.

When Johnny Comes Marching Home

Words and music: Patrick Sarsfield Gilmore.

Grand review at Washington – Sherman veterans marching through Pennsylvania Avenue

When Johnny comes marching home again, Hurrah, Hurrah,
We'll give him a hearty welcome then, Hurrah, Hurrah;
The men will cheer, the boys will shout, the ladies, they will all turn out,
And we'll all feel gay, when Johnny comes marching home.

The old church bells will peal with joy, Hurrah, Hurrah,
To welcome home our darling boy, Hurrah, Hurrah;
The village lads and lassies say, with roses they will strew the way
And we'll all feel gay, when Johnny comes marching home.

Get ready for the Jubilee, Hurrah, Hurrah,
We'll give the hero three times three, Hurrah, Hurrah,
The laurel wreath is ready now, to place upon his loyal brow,
And we'll all feel gay, when Johnny comes marching home.

Let love and friendship on that day, Hurrah, Hurrah,
Their choicest treasures then display, Hurrah, Hurrah,
And let each one perform some part, to fill with joy the warrior's heart,
And we'll all feel gay, when Johnny comes marching home.

The Union Forever

The Last Fierce Charge

Many of the songs of the Civil War, North and South, were sentimental songs - songs of home, sweetheart and mother. Often it is impossible to tell from the words whether the soldier is Union or Confederate.

"The Last Fierce Charge" was passed down through Keith McNeil's family from his great-grandfather Cary Calvin Oakley, a Californian, who learned and sang the song during the Civil War.

The Last Fierce Charge

Words and music: anonymous.

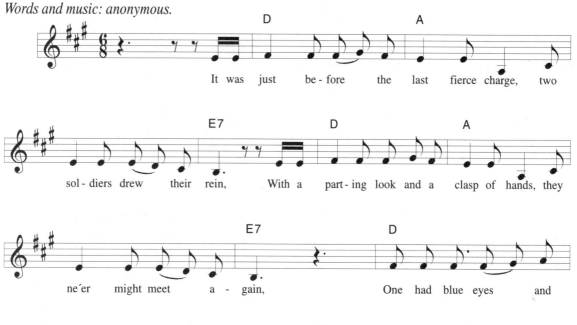

It was just before the last fierce charge, two soldiers drew their rein,
With a parting look and a clasp of hands, they ne'er might meet again,
One had blue eyes and curly hair, nineteen but a month ago,
He had red on his cheek and down on his chin,
he was only a boy, you know.

The other was tall, dark, stern and proud, his faith in life was dim,
He only trusted the more to them who were all the world to him.
The tall dark man was the first to speak,
saying, "Charlie, my time has come,
We'll ride together into the fight, but you'll ride out alone."

"I have a picture on my breast, I will wear it in this fight,
A picture that is all this world to me, and it shines like a morning light,
Like a morning light was her love to me, to brighten my lonely life,
It is care that has caused her furrowed brow,
since she's been my loving wife."

"Write to her tenderly how I died, and where's my resting place;
Tell her in life and even in death, I'll always see her face;
Tell her in heaven I'll wait, in Heaven or earth between.
I'll see her soon, I know I shall, it won't be long I wean."

There were tears in the eyes of the blue-eyed boy,
his voice was filled with pain,
"I'll do my comrade's parting wish, if I ride home again,
But if I should die and you return, will you do as much for me?
I have a fond Mother waits at home, write to her tenderly."

"She's lost all, one by one, husband and sons are gone,
I was the last of all her boys, but she bravely sent me on."
Just then the order came to charge, for an instant hand touched hand,
A last goodbye and on they rode, that brave devoted band.

And though they rode swiftly up the hill, the fight they could not gain,
And the few of those that lived through the fray rode slowly down again;
And among the dead that were left behind was the boy with the curly hair;
The tall dark man that rode by his side lay dead beside him there.

No one to write to the blue-eyed girl the words her lover had said,
Nor a fond Mother waits at home, will know her boy is dead.

Lorena

The favorite sweetheart song of the Confederate soldiers was "Lorena." Lorena came to epitomize all the sweethearts left behind when the soldiers went off to war.

"Lorena" was published in Chicago in 1857, but, like "Dixie," became Southern property.

J. P. Webster, who composed the music, wrote songs during the war in support of the Union cause. His most famous composition was the ever popular hymn "The Sweet Bye and Bye."

Lorena

Words: Rev. H. D. L. Webster. Music: J. P. Webster.

The years creep slow-ly by, Lo-ren-a, the snow is on the grass a-gain; The sun's low down the sky, Lo-ren-a, the frost gleams where the flow'rs have been. But the heart throbs on as warm-ly now, as when the sum-mer days were nigh; Oh! the sun can ne-ver dip so low, a-down af-fec-tion's cloud-less sky, The sun can nev-er slip so low, a-down af-fec-tion's cloud-less sky.

The years creep slowly by, Lorena, the snow is on the grass again;
The sun's low down the sky, Lorena,
the frost gleams where the flowers have been.
But the heart throbs on as warmly now,
as when the summer days were nigh;
Oh! the sun can never dip so low, a-down affection's cloudless sky,
The sun can never slip so low, a-down affection's cloudless sky.

A hundred months have passed, Lorena,
since last I held that hand in mine,
And felt the pulse beat fast, Lorena,
though mine beat faster far than thine.
A hundred months, 'twas flowery May,
when up the hilly slope we climbed,
To watch the dying of the day, and hear the distant church bells chime,
To watch the dying of the day, and hear the distant church bells chime.

We loved each other then, Lorena, more than we ever dared to tell;
And what we might have been, Lorena,
had but our lovings prospered well -
But then, 'tis past, the years are gone,
I'll not call up their shadowy forms;
I'll say to them, "Lost years, sleep on! sleep on!
nor heed life's pelting storms."
I'll say to them, "Lost years, sleep on! sleep on!
nor heed life's pelting storms."

The story of that past, Lorena, alas! I care not to repeat,
The hopes that could not last, Lorena, they lived, but only lived to cheat,
I would not cause e'en one regret to rankle in your bosom now;
For "If we try, we may forget," were words of thine long years ago.
For "If we try, we may forget," were words of thine long years ago.

Yes, these were words of thine, Lorena, they burn within my memory yet;
They touched some tender chords, Lorena, which thrill and tremble with regret.
'Twas not thy woman's heart that spoke; thy heart was always true to me;
A duty, stern and pressing, broke the tie which linked my soul with thee.
A duty, stern and pressing, broke the tie which linked my soul with thee.

It matters little now, Lorena, the past is in the eternal past,
Our heads will soon lie low, Lorena, life's tide is ebbing out so fast,
There is a Future! O, thank God! of life this is so small a part!
'Tis dust to dust beneath the sod! but there, up there, 'tis heart to heart,
'Tis dust to dust beneath the sod! but there, up there, 'tis heart to heart.

Aura Lea

The Union's counterpart to "Lorena" was "Aura Lea."

Aura Lea

Words: W. W. Fosdick, Esq. Music: G. P. Poulton.

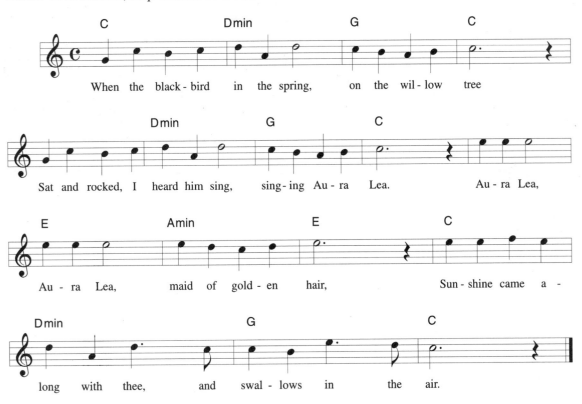

When the black - bird in the spring, on the wil - low tree
Sat and rocked, I heard him sing, sing - ing Au - ra Lea. Au - ra Lea,
Au - ra Lea, maid of gold - en hair, Sun - shine came a -
long with thee, and swal - lows in the air.

When the blackbird in the Spring, on the willow tree
Sat and rocked, I heard him sing, singing Aura Lea.
Aura Lea, Aura Lea, maid of golden hair,
Sunshine came along with thee, and swallows in the air.

In thy blush the rose was born, music when you spake,
Through thine azure eye the morn sparkling seemed to break.
Aura Lea, Aura Lea, birds of crimson wing,
Never song have sung to me as in that sweet, sweet spring.

CHORUS
Aura Lea, Aura Lea, maid of golden hair;
Sunshine came along with thee, and swallows in the air.

Aura Lea! the bird may flee, the willow's golden hair,
Swing through winter fitfully on the stormy air.
Yet if thy blue eyes I see, gloom will soon depart;
For to me, sweet Aura Lea, is sunshine through the heart.

When the mistletoe was green, midst the winter's snows,
Sunshine in thy face was seen, kissing lips of rose.
Aura Lea, Aura Lea, take my golden ring;
Love and light return with thee, and swallows with the spring.

CHORUS
Aura Lea, Aura Lea, maid of golden hair;
Sunshine came along with thee, and swallows in the air.

The Children of the Battlefield

In June, 1863, Confederate General Robert E. Lee invaded Pennsylvania. Lee wanted to shift the Union's effort from capturing Richmond to protecting Washington. He also wanted Northern supplies, hoped to damage Union morale and release the pressure that the Union army was putting on Virginia. Lee's Pennsylvania campaign culminated at Gettysburg, with the most important battle of the war. Robert E. Lee's seemingly invincible Army of Northern Virginia was defeated by General Meade's army on July 3rd, and Lee retreated to Virginia.

After the battle, a dead soldier was found on the battlefield clutching a photograph of his three children. Ballad singer James Clark wrote "The Children of the Battlefield," and the cover of the sheet music featured the original photograph of the children.

The Children of the Battlefield

Words and music: James Gowdy Clark.

gazed with-in a lit-tle frame their pic-tured form to see. And

blame him not if in the strife he breathed a sol-dier's

prayer, "Oh Fa-ther shield the sol - dier's wife, and for his chil - dren

care, And for his chil - dren care."

Upon the field of Gettysburg, the summer sun was high,
When freedom met her haughty foe beneath a Northern sky.
Among the heroes of the North who swelled her grand array
And rushed like mountain eagles forth from happy homes away,
There stood a man of humble fame, a sire of children three,
And gazed within a little frame their pictured form to see.
And blame him not if in the strife he breathed a soldier's prayer,
"Oh Father shield the soldier's wife, and for his children care,
And for his children care."

Upon the field of Gettysburg, when morning shone again,
The crimson cloud of battle burst in streams of fiery rain.
Our legions quelled the awful flood of shot and steel and shell,
While banners marked with ball and blood, around them rose and fell,
And none more nobly won the name of champion of the free,
Than he who pressed the little frame that held his children three.
And none were braver in the strife than he who breathed the prayer,
"Oh, Father shield the soldier's wife, and for his children care,
And for his children care."

Upon the field of Gettysburg, the full moon slowly rose,
She looked and saw ten thousand brows all pale in death's repose.
And down beside a silver stream, from other forms away
Calm as a warrior in a dream our fallen comrade lay,
His limbs were cold, his sightless eyes were fixed upon the three
Sweet stars that rose in memory's skies to light him o'er death's sea.
And honored be the soldier's life, and hallowed be his prayer,
"Oh, Father shield the soldier's wife, and for his children care,
And for his children care."

Robert E. Lee

'Twas at the Siege of Vicksburg

One of the keys to keeping the Confederacy in the war was the 150 mile stretch of Mississippi River still controlled by the South. This area extended from the fortifications at Vicksburg, Mississippi, to those at Port Hudson, Louisiana. Loss of this stretch would cut off the West from the rest of the Confederacy. General Ulysses S. Grant's army kept up a long, continuous siege at Vicksburg. After seven weeks, with food running out, supply lines cut and troops exhausted, Confederate General Pemberton met with Grant to discuss terms of surrender. The day was July 3rd, the same day Lee was defeated at Gettysburg.

During the long siege, Vicksburg residents sang " 'Twas at the Siege of Vicksburg" to the tune "Listen to the Mockingbird."

'Twas at the Siege of Vicksburg

Words: anonymous. Music: Septimus Winner.

'Twas at the siege of Vicksburg,
Of Vicksburg, of Vicksburg,
'Twas at the siege of Vicksburg,
When the Parrot shells were whistling through the air.

CHORUS
Listen to the Parrot shells, listen to the Parrot shells,
The Parrot shells are whistling through the air,
Listen to the Parrot shells, listen to the Parrot shells,
The Parrot shells are whistling through the air.

Oh, well will we remember,
Remember, remember,
Tough mule meat June sans November,
And the Minie balls that whistled through the air.

CHORUS
Listen to the Minie balls, listen to the Minie balls,
The Minie balls are singing in the air,
Listen to the Minie balls, listen to the Minie balls,
The Minie balls are singing in the air.

The Minie balls referred to in the song were bullets. They were easily rammed down the "rifled" barrel (barrels with grooves causing the rifle ball to spin rapidly) because they were of smaller diameter than the barrel. The Minie had a concave base with a wooden cone. When fired, the explosion expanded the lead bullet into the rifling grooves of the barrel. Rifled barrels, developed in the 1850's, improved both accuracy and range.

"Parrot shells" were shells fired from cannons designed by Captain Robert P. Parrot. Parrot's cannons also had rifled barrels.

Interview between Grant and Pemberton

I Goes to Fight mit Sigel

By 1864, between twenty and twenty-five percent of the Union's troops were foreign-born, mostly Irish and German. This dialect song is about a German-American soldier who goes off to fight alongside other German-American troops in the Second Missouri Brigade. The Second Missouri was commanded by General Franz Sigel, a favorite figure in the German-American community.

I Goes to Fight mit Sigel

Words: J. F. Poole. Music: anonymous.

Dem Deutsch - en mens mit Si - gel's band at fight-ing have no ri - val; Und ven Cheff Da-vis mens ve meet, ve schlauch em like de tuy - vil. Dere's on - ly von ting vot I fear, ven pat - tling for der Ea - gle, I von't get not no la - ger beer, ven I goes to fight mit Si - gel.

I've come shust now to tells you how I goes mit regimentals,
To schlauch dem voes of Liberty, like dem old Continentals,
Vot fights mit England long ago, to save der Yankee Eagle;
Und now I gets my soldier clothes, I goes to fight mit Sigel.

Ven I comes from der Deutsche Countree, I vorks somedimes at baking;
Und den I keeps a lager beer saloon, und den I goes shoe-making;
But now I vas a sojer been to save der Yankee Eagle,
To schlouch dem tam secession volks, I goes to fight mit Sigel.

I gets ein tam big rifle guns, und puts him to mine shoulder,
Den march so bold like a big jackhorse, und may been someding bolder;
I goes off mit de volunteers to save der Yankee Eagle;
To give dem Rebel vellers fits, I goes to fight mit Sigel.

Dem Deutschen mens mit Sigel's band at fighting have no rival;
Und ven Cheff Davis mens ve meet, ve schlauch em like de tuyvil.
Dere's only von ting vot I fear, ven pattling for der Eagle,
I von't get not no lager beer, ven I goes to fight mit Sigel.

For rations dey gives salty pork, I dinks dat vas a great sell;
I petter likes de sauerkraut, der Schvitzer-kase und bretzel.
If fighting Joe will give us dem, ve'll save der Yankee Eagle,
Und I'll put mine vrou in Breech-a-loons, to go and fight mit Sigel.

Charles G. Halpine, who served on the staff of Major General David ("Black Dave") Hunter used the popularity of dialect songs to help break down white resistance to enlisting black soldiers. Halpine's pen name was "Private Miles O'Reilly," and one of his songs, "Sambo's Right to Be Kilt," was written for this purpose.

Some tell us 'tis a burnin' shame to make the naygers fight;
An' that the thrade of bein' kilt belongs to but the white;
But as for me, upon my soul! so liberal are we here,
I'll let Sambo be murthered instead of myself on every day of the year.
On every day of the year, boys, and in every hour of the day;
The right to be kilt I'll divide wid him, an' divil a word I'll say.

The men who object to Sambo should take his place and fight;
And it's betther to have a nayger's hue than a liver that's wake an' white.
Though Sambo's black as the ace of spades, his finger a thrigger can pull,
And his eye runs sthraight on the barrel-sights from undher its thatch of wool.
So hear me all, boys darlin', don't think I'm tippin' you chaff,
The right to be kilt we'll divide wid him, and give him the largest half!

Franz Sigel

Old Abe Lincoln Came out of the Wilderness

The political climate was grim for Lincoln as he sought re-election in 1864. The Democrats nominated General George B. McClellan, and instigated a smear campaign against Lincoln, capitalizing on anti-black prejudice. McClellan's supporters described Lincoln's platform as:

"subjugation, emancipation, confiscation, domination, annihilation, destruction - in order to produce miscegenation!"

The situation changed dramatically when, just before the election, General William Tecumseh Sherman captured Atlanta, and Admiral Farragut won an important naval victory in Mobile Bay. The Lincoln-Johnson ticket won 22 of the 25 states in the Union, and the Republicans won a two-thirds majority in Congress.

Sung to the tune "Down in Alabam," "Old Abe Lincoln" was Lincoln's most popular campaign song.

Old Abe Lincoln Came out of the Wilderness

Words and music: J. Warner.

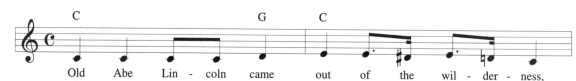

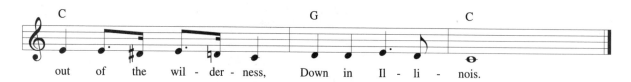

Old Abe Lincoln came out of the wilderness,
Out of the wilderness, out of the wilderness,
Old Abe Lincoln came out of the wilderness,
Down in Illinois.

CHORUS
Down in Illinois, down in Illinois,
Old Abe Lincoln came out of the wilderness
Down in Illinois.

Old Jeff Davis tore down the government,
Tore down the government, tore down the government,
Old Jeff Davis tore down the government,
Many long years ago.

CHORUS
Many long years ago, many long years ago,
Old Jeff Davis tore down the government,
Many long years ago.

Old Abe Lincoln built up a better one,
Built up a better one, built up a better one,
Old Abe Lincoln built up a better one,
Many long years ago.

CHORUS
Many long years ago, many long years ago,
Old Abe Lincoln built up a better one,
Many long years ago.

We Are the Boys of Potomac's Ranks

The lack of a strong two-party system hurt the South. Despite Jefferson Davis's shortcomings as commander-in-chief, there was no way to replace him, or even compel him to change. Lee, his best tactician, wanted to strike hard in Union territory, but Davis refused to appoint a single military officer to oversee command of the Confederate army. He kept that privilege for himself. Each of his generals had to work through him before taking major action, and this hampered the effectiveness of the army.

Lincoln had his problems, too. His strategy was to move on all Southern defensive areas simultaneously, taking advantage of the North's numerical superiority in arms and men. However, none of Lincoln's commanding generals would carry out this strategy. Union soldiers shared Lincoln's frustration. In the fall of 1863, soldiers in the Army of the Potomac sang about the shortcomings of their commanders, to the tune of "When Johnny Comes Marching Home."

Irvin McDowell

Nathaniel P. Banks

We Are the Boys of Potomac's Ranks

Words: anonymous. Music: Patrick S. Gilmore.

We are the boy's of Po-to-mac's ranks, hur-rah, hur-rah, We are the boy's of Po-to-mac's ranks, hur-rah, hur-rah, We are the boy's of Po-to-mac's ranks, We ran with Mc-Dow-ell, re-treat-ed with Banks, And we'll all drink, stone blind, John-ny fill up the bowl.

John Pope

George B. McClellan

Joseph Hooker

Ambrose E. Burnside

George G. Meade

We are the boys of Potomac's ranks, hurrah, hurrah,
We are the boys of Potomac's ranks, hurrah, hurrah,
We are the boys of Potomac's ranks,
We ran with McDowell, retreated with Banks,
And we'll all drink, stone blind, Johnny fill up the bowl.

We fought with McClellan, the Rebs, shakes and fever, hurrah, hurrah,
We fought with McClellan, the Rebs, shakes and fever, hurrah, hurrah,
We fought with McClellan, the Rebs, shakes and fever,
But Mac joined the navy on reaching James River,
And we'll all drink, stone blind, Johnny fill up the bowl.

They gave us John Pope, our patience to tax, hurrah, hurrah,
They gave us John Pope, our patience to tax, hurrah, hurrah,
He said his headquarters were in the saddle,
But Stonewall Jackson made him skedaddle,
And we'll all drink, stone blind, Johnny fill up the bowl.

Then Mac was recalled, but after Antietam, hurrah, hurrah,
Then Mac was recalled, but after Antietam, hurrah, hurrah,
Then Mac was recalled, but after Antietam,
Abe gave him a rest, he was too slow to beat 'em,
And we'll all drink, stone blind, Johnny fill up the bowl.

Old Burnside then he tried his luck, hurrah, hurrah,
Old Burnside then he tried his luck, hurrah, hurrah,
Old Burnside then he tried his luck,
But in the mud, so fast got stuck,
And we'll all drink, stone blind, Johnny fill up the bowl.

Then Hooker was taken to fill the bill, hurrah, hurrah,
Then Hooker was taken to fill the bill, hurrah, hurrah,
Then Hooker was taken to fill the bill,
But he got a black eye at Chancellorsville,
And we'll all drink, stone blind, Johnny fill up the bowl.

Next came General Meade, a slow old plug, hurrah, hurrah,
Next came General Meade, a slow old plug, hurrah, hurrah,
Next came General Meade, a slow old plug,
For he let 'em get away at Gettysburg,
And we'll all drink, stone blind, Johnny fill up the bowl.

Marching Through Georgia

Early in 1864, Lincoln appointed General Ulysses S. Grant as Lieutenant General in command of the Union army, urging Grant to advance all along the line simultaneously. Grant carried out Lincoln's strategy, and defeated the Confederacy.

When General Sherman outlined to General Grant his plan to march through Georgia and the Carolinas to the sea, he said, "This may not be war, but rather statesmanship." Sherman's march was a devastating blow to Southern morale. He took his 65,000 troops and an ever-growing number of contrabands ten miles a day, destroying everything that could be of value to the Confederate army: depots, stores, mills, machine shops, factories, and 300 miles of railroad track. The contrabands, who knew the land, provided invaluable assistance.

"Marching Through Georgia" was one of the most popular songs of the war in the North, and the most hated in the South.

Marching Through Georgia

Words and music: Henry Clay Work.

Bring the good old bugle, boys! we'll sing another song.
Sing it with a chorus that will start the world along,
Sing it as we used to sing it, fifty thousand strong,
While we were marching through Georgia.

CHORUS
"Hurrah! Hurrah! we bring the Jubilee!
Hurrah! Hurrah! the flag that makes you free!"
So we sang the chorus from Atlanta to the sea,
While we were marching through Georgia.

"Sherman's dashing Yankee boys will never reach the coast!"
So the saucy rebels said, 'twas a handsome boast,
Had they not forgot, alas! to reckon with the host,
While we were marching through Georgia.

How the darkeys shouted when they heard the joyful sound!
How the turkeys gobbled which our commissary found!
How the sweet potatoes even started from the ground,
While we were marching through Georgia.

Yes, and there were Union men who wept with joyful tears,
When they saw the honored flag they had not seen for years;
Hardly could they be restrained from breaking forth in cheers,
While we were marching through Georgia.

And so we made a thoroughfare for Freedom and her train,
Sixty miles in latitude, three hundred to the main;
Treason fled before us, for resistance was in vain,
While we were marching through Georgia

   Sherman's march inspired other songs, too,
including "When Sherman Marched down to the Sea."

Proud, proud was our army that morning
That stood by the Cypress and Pine,
Then Sherman said, "Boys, you are weary,
This day fair Savannah is mine!"
Then sang we a song for our chieftain,
That echoed o'er river and sea
And the stars on our banners shone brighter
When Sherman marched down to the sea.

William Tecumseh Sherman

We Are Marching on to Richmond

   Late in 1864, the governors of North Carolina, South Carolina, Georgia, Alabama and Mississippi passed a resolution recommending that blacks serve as soldiers. Urged on by General Lee, the Confederate Congress passed the "Negro Soldier Law" in March, 1865. Two companies of African-American soldiers were organized in Richmond, but it was too late for the Confederacy.

   On April 3, 1865, three Union regiments, one black and two white, entered Richmond. The city that had withstood siege for four long years finally fell to the Union army.

We Are Marching on to Richmond
Words and music: E. W. Locke.

Our knap - sack sling and blithe - ly sing, we're march - ing on to Rich - mond; With weap - ons bright, and hearts so light, we're march - ing on to Rich - mond. Each

Our knapsacks sling and blithely sing, we're marching on to Richmond;
With weapons bright, and hearts so light, we're marching on to Richmond.
Each weary mile with song beguile, we're marching on to Richmond;
The roads are rough but smooth enough, to take us safe to Richmond.

CHORUS
Then tramp away while the bugles play, we're marching on to Richmond;
Our flag shall gleam in the morning beam,
 from many a spire in Richmond.

Our foes are near, their drums we hear,
they're camped about in Richmond;
With pickets out, to tell the route, our army takes to Richmond.
We've crafty foes to meet our blows, no doubt they'll fight for Richmond;
The brave may die but never fly, we'll cut our way to Richmond.

But yesterday, in murderous fray, while marching on to Richmond,
We parted here from comrades dear, while marching on to Richmond;
With manly sighs and tearful eyes, while marching on to Richmond,
We laid the braves in peaceful graves, and started on for Richmond.

Our friends away are sad today, because we march to Richmond;
With loving fears they shrink to hear, about our march to Richmond;
The pen shall tell that they who fell, while marching on to Richmond,
Had hearts aglow and face to foe while marching on to Richmond.

Our thoughts shall roam to scenes of home
while marching on to Richmond,
The vacant chair that's waiting there while we march on to Richmond;
'Twill not be long till shout and song we'll raise aloud in Richmond,
And war's rude blast, will soon be past,
and we'll go home from Richmond.

Ruins of Richmond – Main Street

Tenting on the Old Camp Ground

On April 9th, 1865, at Appomattox, Virginia, Robert E. Lee surrendered to Ulysses S. Grant. Five days later, on April 14th, Abraham Lincoln was assassinated. General Johnston surrendered on April 26th, General Taylor on May 4th. Confederate President Jefferson Davis was captured on May 10th, General Smith surrendered on May 26th and the war was over.

Walter Kittredge, singer, lecturer and composer, wrote "Tenting on the Old Camp Ground" in 1864, when he received his draft notice. After a Boston publisher rejected the song, Kittredge enlisted the help of Asa Hutchinson, of the famous Hutchinson Family Singers, to persuade Oliver Ditson & Company to publish the song. "Tenting on the Old Camp Ground" expressed the feelings of soldiers and civilians, North and South. Its universal appeal continued long after the war, and had a resurgence of popularity among American soldiers who served in the Vietnam War.

Tenting on the Old Camp Ground

Words and music: Walter Kittredge.

We are tent-ing to-night on the old camp ground, give us a song to cheer Our wea-ry hearts, a song of home and friends we love so dear.

Chorus

Man-y are the hearts that are wea-ry to-night, wish-ing for the war to cease; Man-y are the hearts that are look-ing for the right to see the dawn of peace. Tent-ing to-night, tent-ing to-night, tent-ing on the old camp ground.

We are tenting tonight on the old camp ground, give us a song to cheer
Our weary hearts, a song of home and friends we love so dear.

CHORUS
Many are the hearts that are weary tonight, wishing for the war to cease;
Many are the hearts that are looking for the right to see the dawn of peace.
Tenting tonight, tenting tonight, tenting on the old camp ground.

We are tired of war, on the old camp ground, many are dead and gone
Of the brave and true who left their homes, others been wounded long.

We've been fighting today on the old camp ground,
Many are lying near. Some are dead, some are dying, others are in tears.

LAST CHORUS
Many are the hearts that are weary tonight, wishing for the war to cease;
Many are the hearts that are looking for the right to see the dawn of peace.
Dying tonight, dying tonight, dying on the old camp ground.

Blue-Gray Medley

The Civil War was America's costliest war. With a population of less than thirty million people, more than half a million soldiers died. Two thirds died from starvation and disease and one third were killed in battle. Two out of three of the dead were Union soldiers.

The cost was about three and a half billion dollars for the North, and two billion for the South. The war strengthened the Northern economy, and nearly destroyed the Southern economy.

The social cost in bitterness, hatred, misunderstanding and prejudice was beyond measure.

"Blue-Gray Medley" is arranged for two clarinets.

Blue-Gray Medley

Position of the Confederate Army when the surrender was announced

Recommended sources for and about songs sung during the Civil War:

Bernard, Kenneth A. *Lincoln and the Music of the Civil War*. Caldwell, Ohio: Caxton Printers, 1966.

Crawford, Richard. *The Civil War Songbook*. New York: Dover Publications, Inc., 1977.

Dolph, Edward Arthur. *"Sound Off" Soldier Songs*. New York: Cosmopolitan Book Corp., 1929.

Fowke, Edith and Glazer, Joe. *Songs of Work and Freedom*. Chicago: Roosevelt University, 1960.

Garofalo, Robert and Elrod, Mark. *A Pictorial History of Civil War Era Musical Instruments & Military Bands*. Charleston, West Virginia: Pictorial Histories Publishing Company, 1985.

Glass, Paul and Singer, Louis C. *Singing Soldiers*. New York: Da Capo Press, Inc., 1975.

Harwell, Richard B. *Confederate Music*. Chapel Hill, North Carolina: The University of North Carolina Press, 1950.

Heaps, Willard A. and Porter W. *The Singing Sixties - The Spirit of Civil War Days Drawn from the Music of the Times*. Norman, Oklahoma: University of Oklahoma Press, 1960.

Higginson, Thomas Wentworth. *Army Life in a Black Regiment*. Boston: Beacon Press, 1962.

Howe, Julia Ward. *Reminiscences 1819 - 1899*. Boston: Houghton, Mifflin and Company, 1899.

Jordan, Philip D. *Singin' Yankees*. Minneapolis: The University of Minnesota Press, 1946.

Levy, Lester S. *Flashes of Merriment: A Century of Humorous Songs in America*. Norman, Oklahoma: University of Oklahoma Press, 1971.

Luther, Frank. *Americans and Their Songs*. New York: Harper & Brothers Publishers, 1942.

Marsh, J. B. T. *The Story of the Jubilee Singers; With Their Songs*. Boston: Houghton, Osgood and Company, 1880.

Scott, John Anthony. *The Ballad of America*. New York: Bantam Books, Inc., 1966.

Silber, Irwin. *Songs of the Civil War*. New York: Columbia University Press, 1960.

Work, John W. *American Negro Songs and Spirituals*. New York: Bonanza Books, 1940.

Picture Credits

The pictures in this volume were taken from *Harper's Pictorial History of the Great Rebellion in the United States*, by Alfred H. Guernsey and Henry M. Alden, 1866, and from *Harper's Pictorial History of the Great Rebellion in the United States, Part Second*, by Alfred H. Guernsey and Henry M. Alden, 1868. The publisher later changed the titles to *Harper's Pictorial History of the Civil War*.

Index of songs

Abraham's Daughter 28
Alabama, The 72
Alabama, The (Northern version) 73
All Quiet Along the Potomac Tonight 2
Answer to Maryland, My Maryland....................11
Army Bean, The 46
Army Bugs 47
Army Grub 45
Aura Lea 85
Battle Cry of Freedom, The 40
Battle Cry of Freedom, The (Northern soldiers' parody) .42
Battle Hymn of the Republic, The 37
Battle of Shiloh Hill, The 39
Blue-Gray Medley (arranged for two clarinets) 100
Bonnie Blue Flag, The 13
Bonnie White Flag, The 78
Children of the Battlefield, The 86
Come in out of the Draft 53
Cumberland and the *Merrimac*, The 70
Cumberland Crew, The 71
Dixie's Land 14
Dixie parody (Arkansas) 16
Dixie parody (Texas) 17
Ellsworth Avengers 30
For Bales 56
Free at Last 65
Frémont Train, The 4
Go Down Moses 63
God Save the South 9
Goober Peas 43
Hard Crackers Come Again No More 44
Homespun Dress, The 48
How Are You, John Morgan? 75
I Goes to Fight mit Sigel 90
John Brown's Body 66
John Brown's Body (Sojourner Truth's parody) 69
Just Before the Battle, Mother 32

Just Before the Battle, Mother (Southern parody) 33
Kentucky, Oh Kentucky 74
Kingdom Coming 58
Last Fierce Charge, The 82
Lincoln and Liberty 5
Lorena 83
Marching Song of the First Arkansas Regiment, The 68
Marching Through Georgia 95
Maryland, My Maryland 10
May that Cuss, Jeff Davis Float 79
No More Auction Block for Me 60
Oh, Freedom 62
Old Abe Lincoln Came out of the Wilderness 92
Riding a Raid 34
Sambo's Right to be Kilt 91
Slavery Chain Done Broke at Last 61
Southern Battle Cry of Freedom, The 41
Southern Marseillaise, The 20
Southern Wagon, The 6
Stonewall Jackson's Way 36
Tenting on the Old Camp Ground 98
Tramp! Tramp! Tramp! 77
Treasury Rats 24
'Twas at the Siege of Vicksburg 88
Virginia Marseillaise, The 20
We Are Coming, Father Abraham 50
We Are Coming, Father Abraham,
    Three Hundred Dollars More 54
We Are Marching on to Richmond 96
We Are the Boys of Potomac's Ranks 93
What's the Matter? 23
When Johnny Comes Marching Home 80
When Sherman Marched down to the Sea 96
Yankee Cheesebox on a Raft, A 71
Yankee Doodle (setting for Highland bagpipe) 26
Yellow Rose of Texas, The 19

Acknowledgements

We would like to extend our thanks to Darrin Schuck for his work on the musical notation of the songs. Our valuable historians and song-finders included Barbara Critchlow, Ken Gates and T. E. Foreman, as well as reference librarians at the Library of Congress and the Lincoln Center of the Smiley Library in Redlands, California. Our grateful thanks for editing and proofreading go to Mary McNeil Cheever and Connie McNeil, and to John Garrett Short for design work and layout. We are also indebted to Keith's mother, Marion Oakley McNeil, now deceased, who taught him many of the songs.